VALUES AND IMPERATIVES

Clarence Irving Lewis

VALUES AND IMPERATIVES

STUDIES IN ETHICS

Edited by John Lange

STANFORD UNIVERSITY PRESS

STANFORD, CALIFORNIA

1969

Stanford University Press
Stanford, California
© 1969 by the Board of Trustees of the
Leland Stanford Junior University
Printed in the United States of America
L. C. 69-13181

Preface

There are a number of people who have, to one degree or another, helped to bring this book about. Most prominent among these are Professors Charles A. Baylis and William K. Frankena, of Duke University and the University of Michigan respectively. Their recommendations, advice, and encouragement have been consistently valuable and heartening. It would be difficult to express the extent of my appreciation for their generous and unfailing support and counsel. Outside the philosophical community I am particularly indebted to Mr. Andrew K. Lewis, one of Professor Lewis's sons and the executor of the C. I. Lewis Estate, for making available microfilms and xeroxed copies of his father's late papers, and supplying me with information and helping me with an abundant miscellany of problems that would be too prodigious to recount, or remember.

For particular favors or bits of information I would like to express my gratitude to Professors John D. Goheen of Stanford University, G. H. von Wright of the Academy of Finland, John F. A. Taylor and William J. Callaghan, both of Michigan State University, Frederick Sontag of Pomona College, Roy Wood Sellars, Professor Emeritus of the University of Michigan, and Priscilla P. Leonard, wife of the late Professor Henry S. Leonard of Michigan State University.

The chronology of the papers in this volume is as follows: The lectures "Foundations of Ethics" were delivered at Wesleyan University in 1959. "Values and Facts" was prepared in about 1952 for a cooperative volume on value to be edited by Professors Roy Wood Sellars and Sidney Hook, but the volume never appeared. "Pragmatism and the Roots of the Moral" was delivered at Pomona College in 1956. "Practical and Moral Imperatives" was delivered at Swarthmore College in 1949. "The Meaning of Liberty" appeared in the *Revue Internationale de Philosophie*, No. 6, in 1948, and is reprinted here with the permission of the publishers of that journal. "The Rational Imperatives" appeared in 1953 in the anthology *Vision and Action: Essays in Honor of Horace M. Kallen on His 70th Birthday*, edited by Sidney Ratner, and published by Rutgers University Press, which has granted its permission to reprint it here. "The Categorical Imperative" was originally delivered at Michigan State University in 1958.

J.L.

Contents

Introduction

I do not much care for introductions, and when not in a peculiarly conscientious or compulsive mood delight in the healthy saneness of skipping them. However, when one has put together a number of writings, one finds oneself sorely tempted to say something about them, a temptation to which one will likely succumb, as in the present case.

C. I. Lewis was a great philosopher, and a great man, and I think there are very few people about, of any philosophical or political persuasion, of whom this can be truly said. Perhaps that is the most important thing to be said in this introduction, the simplest thing, and the truest.

But I think there is little doubt that these papers will, on the whole, be received with distinctly mixed responses in the philosophical community. I hope that will be the case, for they have edges. About this matter and certain related matters I think something should be said.

Only two of the papers—"The Rational Imperatives" and "The Meaning of Liberty"—have appeared previously in print. Most of the papers included here are lectures and, as such, were not intended for publication. An exception to this is "Values and Facts," prepared for a cooperative volume on value once projected by Professors Sidney Hook and Roy Wood Sellars, which was never completed. We do have evidence, however, that Lewis was willing to print the set of lectures "Foundations of Ethics," which begins this volume. They were to be printed in the event that he was unable to finish the major contribution to ethics to which he devoted his last years. That Lewis did not live to finish this work is one of the tragedies of philosophy. It exists now as a set of gleaming fragments which will certainly never see print as Lewis would have wished, if they see print at all. Accordingly it is all the more important that the four lectures "Foundations of Ethics" be printed. I think that most readers will find them a valuable presentation, in small scope, of most of the central theses of Lewis's ethics. They are, to my mind at least, superior to his *The Ground and Nature of the Right* and *Our Social Inheritance*.

The three remaining papers were all public lectures and were not, as far as we know, written for publication, even conditional publication, as might be considered the case with "Foundations of Ethics." Yet each of them seems to me to illuminate some aspect of Lewis's thinking on ethical matters. For example, "Practical and Moral Imperatives" indicates the lines which Lewis took, and would presumably still take, at least substantially, in responding to valued and significant criticism pertaining to the difficulties of grounding a theory of obligation in a naturalistic matrix; and that paper, as well, gives us some light, not much, on the extremely important but never fully developed notion of the pragmatic *a priori* as applied to the problems of morality. "Pragmatism and the Roots of the Moral," clearly recognizable as a predecessor of the four lectures "Foundations of Ethics," makes clear not only Lewis's notion of the compatibility of pragmatism with moral rigor, but more importantly, his conviction that only in the pragmatically nonrepudiable vocation of the acting and thinking animal can the principles of a plausible objective morality be founded; in spite of its relation to the more recent lectures, it seems to me worthy of being made independently available to the philosophical community. Finally, "The Categorical Imperative" gives us Lewis discussing Kant, and relating, at some length, his own conception of ethical imperatives to that of Kant, an occasion of interest, one supposes, from anyone's point of view. The responsibility, incidentally, for the selection of papers appearing here is fully mine, though I gratefully acknowledge the advice and help of others, in particular Professors Charles A. Baylis and William K. Frankena. The point of this remark is that if some should feel that certain of the papers here published are not worthy of Lewis, I wish it to be understood that any criticism should be directed at me. Lewis, however, now belongs to philosophy. And even a roughly chipped insight of his, inadequately developed, may have value. If Lewis has seen something, his description is a report, tentative though it may be, which is worth investigating. The touchstone for decision on printing these papers has not been whether Lewis would have let them out of his office but whether, in my opinion, we can profit from them. Lastly, I might remark that there is a fair amount of repetition among certain papers here, but I considered this preferable to slicing them up, or forgetting about them. Lewis tended to return to similar themes, and his entire philosophy, I believe, is best understood as an unfolding, or gradual development and elaboration, of certain fundamental philosophical commitments, naturalistic in temperament, rationalistic in aspect, pragmatic in methodology. This being the case I am ready to meet Epimenides around more than one corner, even if he has the Cyrenaics with him.

The primary reason these papers—considered as a whole—will have a mixed reception in the philosophical community—more so than the standard mixed reception, without which we might be inclined to suspect that the work was not philosophical—is not that these papers, or some of them, do not give us Lewis at his tiptop best, or that they contain repetitions, or that they were on the whole intended for nonphilosophers, which is true, but rather that Lewis is skilled at making people mad.

Something should be said about this, and certainly will, but as a prelude, particularly intended for young philosophers who have not yet sewn themselves into the philosophical uniforms being issued today, I would like to mention that Lewis —as they will discover—reads like Lewis, and not someone else. His notions of philosophy and its methodology were not externally imposed. If one has been trained to think that philosophy reads like Carnap, or Wittgenstein, or Austin, one may not think that Lewis reads like philosophy. This difficulty is not insurmountable, of course, but merely requires the recognition that philosophy is a big country and her lovers come in all shapes and sizes, and that Lewis just happens to have, for this time and place, an unusual shape and size, indeed, perhaps for any time and place. I can recall wondering—several years ago when I was a graduate student listening to Lewis—if he were twenty years behind the times, or twenty in front of them. I'm inclined now to think that he is neither—that only the periphery of his work can be dated, and that the substance has little respect for calendars. Lewis, like Hume and Kant, will be a philosopher whom men who consider the issues of our discipline will, generation after generation, this one or the next, or the one following, return to visit. Thus if it should upon occasion seem that Lewis upsets familiar apple carts, jumps out of ruts, does things which we are told can't be done—*e.g.*, discuss human experience directly, worry about the meanings behind words—and in general fails to follow the standard road maps, the outlines of which are reasonably clear in leading journals, convention programs, etc., I think there is little advice better than the simple encouragement to remain calm: to listen, to try to understand, and if you feel that he has not said it right, to try to say it right yourself. But your criticism, your thinking, if it is to be fair to Lewis and yourself, must be your own, true to yourself, as his was to him. Write what you love, and the devil take the hindmost.

Now about Lewis the irascible.

I myself have boiled a bit on occasion as I felt some pleasant idea of which I was quite fond dismissed by Lewis, properly or improperly, as rubbish. Sometimes it is difficult to escape the suspicion that Lewis's zest to charitably understand his opponents may be overcome in the final analysis by the main object, which is apparently to pulverize them. When Lewis thought that something was a mistake, or an aberration, or an egregious (a favorite word with him) fallacy, he was not the last to let us know about it. This tendency to be somewhat less than deferent with what he regarded as error, occasionally preposterous error, is perhaps a fault, but if so it is one the scale of which in Lewis has a certain awe-inspiring sublimity. At any rate Lewis never practiced the urbane, backhand slap, currently fashionable, but walked up to people and smashed them in the nose. And, of course, if Lewis is *right* in what he says, and I think he may be, at least in large outline, then we are indebted to him for his critique, and perhaps can even acknowledge the justice of its ferocity. The intensity of Lewis's feelings in these matters—the main enemy being ethical noncognitivism—is a reflection of his human concerns. He was a man who felt very deeply about things—with a depth that might be alien and perhaps offensive to some of our parlor philosophers. Philosophy was never a game to Lewis, linguistic or otherwise. It was one of the most important things a human being could do, and one that every human being, in one fashion or another, had to do. The right and the good were as significant and real for Lewis, and as much a part of life and its meaning, as hunger or thirst or kindness or shelter, or any of the economic and humane realities that condition what men are and may become. Accordingly, sensing that our times were ones of confusion and cynicism, of unreflecting fanaticism on the one hand and a flight to the immorality of mechanistic professionalism on the other, Lewis cried out in protest, and wrote his indictments with a pen that was, though it was that of a philosopher, no stranger to passion. In his later years he wanted to write for the general intellectual public—to make a difference in the world, a difference for the right and the good—that could not be made in private dialogues with philosophical rivals, lost in the proliferating, largely unread journals of the discipline. Lewis, in my opinion, owes no one an apology. He would give none in this matter, and I will make none for him.

But far more than for his critique of alternative positions we are indebted to Lewis for what was always his chief glory —his incomparable constructive work, his attempt to build a philosophical statement that would do justice to the valid, the good, and the right, his attempts to tell the truth about what matters most to men. Here, in these papers, and in his other writings, we see the emerging shape of a significant exposition and defense of a reflective common-sense morality, the power of which may render it classical. "Philosophical truth, like knowledge in general," wrote Lewis long ago, "is about experience, and not about something strangely beyond the ken of man, open only to the seer and the prophet. We all know the nature of life and of the real, though only with exquisite care can we tell the truth about them." Lewis was, of course, never satisfied with his own work, and he was particularly distressed that he had not been able to state to his own satisfaction his ethical position, fully grounded in logical, epistemological, and metaphysical considerations. Accordingly these papers indicate rather than delineate his thinking in these matters.

In their way they sketch a blueprint of normative possibilities, the conceptual promise of an edifice he did not live to build, and which perhaps, because of the subtleties, the vastness of the issues involved, no man will ever, or could ever, build; in this, if Lewis has failed, he did so well, leaving behind him the stones for a stairway that was once intended to reach the stars, to attain and touch truthfully on what is most dear to men, what would answer most honestly, most adequately, to the highest sense of what they can be.

We are called by the truth and impassioned by the moral imperative.

Lewis, as few men, has sought the one and adhered fixedly to the other.

FOUNDATIONS OF ETHICS

Ethics and the Present Scene

Ethics may well claim to be the oldest branch of learning. A human being with no group to which he belongs would be an anomaly if not a contradiction. And a human group with no mores which it preserves and inculcates would likewise be imaginary if not impossible. Man himself is a creature of his social organization: without it, he hardly could have survived as a species, and certainly could not have achieved the position of dominance he occupies, regarding this small planet on which he lives as his property, to be administered by him and for the benefit of humankind. Nor could he have attained that level at which his life may now be lived without the complex social structure which distinguishes his species. This social order, in all departments of it, depends upon the continuing social memory and the inheritance of ideas, by which whatever is learned and proves to be of profit for purposes men hold in common is preserved and handed on from one generation to the next. The cumulative traditions so perpetuated—of the sciences, of each art and craft, of political institutions and the law, of economic organization for the division of labor and the exchange of goods—such are the social instrumentalities without which man could not have become what he is, and the progressive character of the civilization he creates would never have been possible.

And the ethics of any group is the cement which holds it together, that part of its continuing tradition which concerns the sanctioned and supported practices by which its cooperation is preserved and made effective. Upon that, all the rest depends. The ethos is the mother of civilization, and the precondition of that progress which the history of man alone among the animals exhibits. The moral tradition is the informing matrix of this historic process, and remains as the arbiter and critique which alone can hold it steady in the direction it is to take. Any ethic may itself alter, develop, and progress, along with that civilization it serves to guide; but if man should ever outgrow his basic sense of mutual obligation in relations with his fellows, then he will stand in danger of destroying all he has achieved and returning to the dust from which he sprang.

For the individual, ethics is among the most important of all modes of learning because it addresses itself to the most frequent and the most exigent of his problems—to the problem, namely, of what he should choose to do. That question is universal to all men and to all occasions on which what they may decide will make any real difference. The only other manner of inquiry which is thus all-pervasive of our living is the question of what we should think—the question of fact or justified belief. And this second question, of the commitment of belief to be taken, is already involved in the question of our doing. There can be no occasion on which what one should choose to do is independent of the circumstances of the case, and of that which, in these circumstances to be met, the action considered will bring about. To act, in the human sense of action, is impossible without reference to what lies within our cognizance—to what we take to be the fact and what we can expect. Whatever is done in the sense of choosing to do is

4

something determined in the light of what we think and believe; it is done deliberately. And without that root of it in our thinking, anything we might be said to do will lack the significance of an act: it will be attributable to us only in that same sense in which we also say that flowers bloom and the wind blows and a compass points to the north. Without our thought and determination behind it, it may be our behavior, but it is not our will which is made manifest; it is not *we* who bring it about.

In turn, however, the significance which attaches to our thinking is one to be fully realized only in what we do. Whatever we may think and come to believe, if our so thinking should have no influence on any decision of action and never eventuate in anything we do, then that thinking would be inconsequential—literally. Doing without thinking is blind; but thinking without doing is idle. It is only in the combination of the two—in what we think and what we do by reason of that thinking—that we are in any wise effective. What a man may do deliberately is all that it lies within his power to control or influence; it represents his total impact on the world he lives in. Except for his encumbering the earth, it is all he counts for, all the difference he will ever make.

Also this question of what to do is that kind of problem which, once it is posed, no man can escape facing and resolving. Only the animal all of whose behavior "does itself," as automatic response to stimulation, can escape decision of acts which are open to him. The creature endowed with the capacity to do by choosing is obliged to exercise it. He *must* decide: the event depends upon his determination of it; and even if he choose to do nothing in this case, the world thereafter will be just a little different by reason of that decision than if he had chosen otherwise.

5

However, it would be dubious to take this whole topic of self-government at large as the province of ethics. As we commonly think of it at least, ethics is concerned with a narrower and more specific question—what we should do toward others, what is to be done in view of our social relationships and of the fact that what one chooses to bring about will have its effect upon one's fellows. And the more comprehensive topic of deliberate doing generally and in all departments of it might better be called Practical Philosophy or the Philosophy of Practice. However, if we look for any well-developed discipline which could be so named and would be adequate to this wider topic of Practical Philosophy, we find that there is none, and that there hardly has been any systematic attempt upon it. That should surprise us, should it not? Here is a subject which is relevant as often as we deliberately do anything, and there is only one part of it, called ethics, which has ever been well studied! This will appear all the more anomalous in view of the fact that men have always understood that there are other indispensable directives of their doing beside those which are denominated *moral*. There are all the various arts and crafts, each with its own set of precepts, observance of which is essential to its successful prosecution. And there is the indispensable advice of prudence, not to be confused with the moral since the prudential and the moral so often are at odds with one another.

The explanation of this anomaly is not too difficult, however, once our attention is drawn to it. But it may be worth a little spelling out, for the sake of the light which can so be thrown on ethics. If there are these different senses of the right to do, and these different departments of the critique of action—the moral, the prudential, and all the diverse modes of technical assessment—then, inevitably, there arises the question of the relation of them to one another, and particularly the question of precedence among them. We have to remember that, on any occasion calling for decision, there will be just one act which is to be chosen and initiated, and just one set of consequences which will so be brought about; and all the various critical considerations which make claim upon this act to be decided must be brought together and focused upon this single occasion which confronts us and the single decision to be made. If, for example, an act can be prudentially sanctioned but morally contraindicated, or morally justified but technically a wrong thing to do, or dictated by technical principles of practice but morally oblique, then it will have to be settled which mode of such critical judgment it is which determines whether the act ought to be done—or whether all are to be given weight, and if so, how their respective claims are to be adjudicated, how they are to be composed in arriving at a single decision, and how any conflict of them is to be obviated.

But that, you will think, is no great problem: it is the moral assessment which must in any case prevail. The moral dictate, as Kant said, is categorical: no if or but about it. Other considerations notwithstanding, what is not *morally* right simply is not right to do. I am disposed to agree. But our agreeing that the moral is the unqualified and final determinant of what it is right to do plainly calls for a somewhat different conception of the moral than that which is likely to be offered if we ask what it means to say that an act is morally right. We shall hardly conceive of the moral judgment as such a final arbitrament unless we also think of it as a judgment in which *all* valid claims upon the act in question are duly weighed and adjudicated. And the technical and prudential, as well as consideration of the consequences to others, are such valid claims.

Instead of any long discussion here, let me simply offer two

7

commonplace examples intended to bring out the point I have in mind. The first of these is meant to illustrate the fact that any relevant technical rightness of an action is essential to its being morally right—or even prudentially right.

Suppose the question is one of the investment of money. Investment is a technical matter in which bankers and brokers require to be expert but any one of us may be called upon to exercise such amateur competence as he commands. Right investment will be a prudential question if it is one's own money the value of which is to be conserved, but it will be a moral question if it should be the money of another for whom one is trustee. But an investment which should be made with deliberate disregard of the technical principles of sound investment would be neither prudentially nor morally right. And this sort of thing will obviously be true in the case of any other manner of technique which should be pertinent to an act considered. No act can be either prudentially right or morally right if, in the doing of it, the principles of any mode of technical rightness which is relevant are deliberately contravened or disregarded. And no final determination of any act will be justified if, in the decision of it, any pertinent technical rightness or wrongness of it should fail to be duly weighed.

The relation of the prudential to the moral is a more complex and difficult matter, concerning which there is much more needing to be said than we should pause to say here in these introductory remarks. I attempt only to suggest the vital point that no decision of action can be moral, in the sense of being the finally right arbitrament, if relevant prudential considerations are ignored. Suppose that I have promised to take part in an important conference, but now, as the time approaches, I find myself suddenly and seriously ill. I still could attend, and could concentrate sufficiently to participate in the discussion. And promises made constitute an obligation to others. Ought I to go, or will it be sufficient if I send my excuses? The common sense of it is that it depends on the relative importance of my possible contribution and, on the other side, upon the seriousness of the possible consequences of my attending in disregard of illness. There are occasions which call for stern subordination of the prudential, and there are others on which that would be uncalled for and unreasonable. And the general conclusion suggested is that no decision is fully justified if taken in complete disregard of any prudential consideration which it may affect. We must not think here that my illness cancels what would otherwise have been my obligation to others. That fudges what is precisely the question: if it is to be said that morally right action is simply doing one's duty to others, can it be further said that a duty to others is determinable without regard to what might be called one's duty to oneself—the prudential? The common sense of the matter, mentioned above, calls for us to answer "No" to this last question.

If you are prepared to accept what my little examples are intended to suggest, then in retrospect we may see a reason why we do not find any well-developed and comprehensive subject to be called Practical Philosophy, separate from Ethics. Ethics, as the topic of that arbitrament of doing which is to be final, and its directives unqualifiedly imperative to follow, cannot fail to claim the whole subject of our self-governed conduct as its field, and attempt to compose and adjudicate *all* valid claims upon our deliberated acts. It must extend to the technically right and to the prudentially right because to ignore what the success of our intentions will require—the technical—or to ignore the doer's own interests—the prudential—would be as unjustified as to ignore the interests of others. At most we can only say that there are wider and narrower senses of the words 'moral' and 'ethics': the narrower connoting peculiar concern with justice to others, and the wider connoting the status of moral judgment as that last and comprehensive assessment of action to which any other manner of its critical advisement must be subordinate. Any full discussion of ethics in this wider sense would be a very large order; but perhaps an ethics which should accept any less inclusive assignment would thereby prejudice correctness within its smaller and acknowledged field.

But if this makes ethics out to be too comprehensive for any adequate treatment, then I have to confess that, quite the contrary, it is still too narrow to include everything which any book with "Ethics" on the cover is almost bound to discuss. As is sometimes emphasized nowadays, the *content* of ethics, strictly taken, consists simply of moral precepts; and there could be—even though there is not—a book entitled "The Moral Code" which should be so compiled that anyone wishing to know what the moral law dictates in a particular case could find out by referring to this book and drawing the proper inferences from what it somewhere says. The parallel to the civil law may be helpful here. For example, California is what is called a code-law state: there is a book—or set of books—in which what is the law is, supposedly, completely set forth; and if you wish to know whether some manner of action is legally right in California, then that is—again, supposedly—inferable from something set down in this legal code.

But even in California we sometimes raise a further question: this is the law; the code dictates it; but is it just; ought it to be the law? Is this legal prescription right? And if the moral law were to be codified and its prescriptions written down, there would likewise be this further question: but is this moral prescription—any particular moral prescription here set forth—right? With respect to the moral, as with respect to any other specific directive of action, one can always raise this second kind of question: is this *directive* justified; is it valid? And—as I am sure you will agree—for any thoughtful individual, and for any organized group, there will be occasions on which that kind of question will be raised, and not only will be but ought to be or even must be.

Otherwise put, we can ask, and must ask, on any occasion calling for deliberate action: what is it that will be right to do? And the answer to that may be given by citing a precept covering this case. But any answer to this first question of what to do being so given, we can ask the second question: but *is* this prescription covering the case a right prescription? *Why* is it right? How does one *know* that this is the right way to decide the matter? How is one to know whether a precept put forward is one which genuinely ought to be followed? And this second question of the validity of precepts or principles becomes inevitable if there can be dispute about the first question of what it is right to do—if one of us can be convinced that a certain manner of meeting the occasion or a certain precept formulating that way of acting is a valid dictate, and conformity to it is morally prescribed, while another of us may be equally convinced that this way of acting and this dictate is not valid and ought not to be followed. If there is no "why" about particular precepts, then there is nothing to which we can appeal in the case of such difference of conviction as to what is right, and no way in which we can tell the difference between a genuinely binding moral dictate and one which merely reflects some unexamined bias or unreasoned sentiment—or some grotesque superstition of a reader of tea leaves.

Let us remember that such irrational ways of telling what it is right to do have had their day and even survive in odd corners of our civilized society.

Also, this second question of the "why" of any particular way of right doing being raised, we can generalize it, or even must generalize it, and consider it in advance of, and apart from, any particular disagreement as to what is right, and any particular precept in question. We can ask ourselves: *Whatever* it is that it is right to do, what makes it so? What constitutes the rightness of it? How can one tell whether a way of acting or a particular precept of action is genuinely right or not? What is the ground on which such a question of right principles can be settled? And unless there is some manner in which we can so distinguish between precepts it is genuinely imperative to adhere to and spurious ones which may be put forward, then it becomes utterly obscure how any difference of conviction regarding right and wrong could possibly be resolved. There must be some criterion for distinguishing between valid dictates of the right and baseless claims that may be made upon our conduct: otherwise the distinction between right and wrong is itself illusory.

None of us needs to be told that it is in fact this second question concerning the ground of moral principles and the manner of their assurance, rather than the contentual principles of ethics themselves, which is the most frequently and extensively discussed topic concerning ethics at the present time. That is also the topic which we here address. I should like to devote the remainder of the present lecture to some general considerations which affect that undertaking.

Perhaps the first question is: Why undertake it? Why not proceed directly to the principles of morals themselves, instead of spending time on these prolegomena to inquiry concerning them? If you make that a personal question, I shall be quite willing to state my mind in the matter—with the understanding that I claim no broader base of information and understanding with respect to it, nor any greater degree of objectivity, than any of us may have. Ethics is everybody's business, not one for experts; and the present scene is as open to the inspection of any one of us as to another. I but put my thoughts before you for consideration.

I feel that if there is any one period more than another in the history of our civilization in which moral clarity and firmness is called for, probably this is it. And I seem to find that, instead of such clarity and firmness, with respect to our values and our apprehension of the basic validities, the present period —among those who are called intellectuals at least—is peculiarly one of confusion and of doubt regarding any basic justification of what we do, the attitudes we should adopt, and the principles we should announce and stand by. Such doubt of the moral validities is widely prevalent in current philosophy, and the disposition to eschew all questions of basic values—as more than social phenomena characterizing particular cultures—extends also to much which the social sciences would currently offer. It is even felt by some that to intrude such questions of the validity of values or of mores marks any social study as unscientific. Instead we are supposed, in order to be scientific, to restrict ourselves to merely descriptive generalizations concerning behavior, perhaps to be illuminated by comparison of human behavior with that of other animals, or examined in the light of the psychology and psychiatry of motivation, or of experiments in the alteration of responses by conditioning. We can make good use of any enlightenment afforded by such generalizations concerning the factual behavior of individuals and of groups, but—as already indicated—no amount of it will either obviate or answer the simple and unavoidable question "What should I do?" As often as we decide our action, that question must be met: there is no alternative, and it cannot be turned into any other and different one. After we are all done with analyzing and explaining ourselves to ourselves, that direct question is still there, and has to be faced in its original and simple form.

It is to be observed that any social scientist who so interprets his task, with respect to mores, as limited to reporting them and finding causal explanation of their being held, omits precisely what those who do *accept and support* any moral principles would offer as the reason for their doing so. Those who hold to them do so from conviction that they are justified, valid, right. They also believe that they have a ground, on which it is imperative to adhere to and support them. But this social scientist I here speak of omits both the first and the second questions of any ethics he examines: what it is in fact right to do and how what is right is to be determined in case there is difference of conviction. He ignores both the questions which those who hold to any ethics will regard as the important ones to ask and answer concerning them. And if such a social scientist further insists that only *his* kind of question about morals is scientific and admits of a scientific answer—with the implication that what is not science is comparatively unimportant—then he gives aid and comfort to the moral cynic, even if he is not himself thus cynical.

I shall not argue here as to the legitimacy or illegitimacy of using the word 'science' in this narrow and invidious manner, which excludes the normative, the questions of ought and ought to be, in contrast to questions merely of what *is*. But I will observe in passing that if the normative questions should come to be neglected, in institutions of higher learning, on account of such usage of a word—'science'—then it becomes dubious where those who are to take the lead in the direction of our social policies, in coming generations, will get the training they will need to have if our civilization is to go forward instead of being brought to a halt or retrogressing.

But let us return to what is material for our discussion. It is some answer to this second question of the ground and validity of moral principles which is presumed in presenting anything in the way of rules of conduct to be accepted and adhered to. Positive ethics is the critique of deliberate doing; but when it is moral principles themselves which are put in doubt, it is a different kind of critical examination which is called for. It is some ground of them, some criterion for distinguishing those which are to be accepted as valid from any whose claim upon us would be spurious and acceptance of which would be a mistake, some answer to the question "How do you know that what this principle dictates is imperative to do?"—which alone could dispel the doubt so raised or decide the issue to be met. The validity of ethics in general—of any ethics—presumes that there is some answer to this kind of question. And it is unclarity about this matter of the foundation on which moral principles rest which leaves all questions of morals open to the skeptical doubt and to the cynical attack.

Strictly, this topic does not belong to ethics itself, and discussions of it have been variously labeled metaphysic of ethics, ethical theory, moral philosophy, and—currently—metaethics. I think it may be helpful to us, in understanding what is involved in it, and the manner in which the questions to which it is addressed will have to be met, if we note first that there is nothing which is peculiar to ethics in this fact that there is such a correlative metastudy, directed to questions of the ground on which and the criteria by which the contents of the branch of study in question are to be attested and assured as valid. There is such a metastudy, often called theory-of or philosophy-of, correlative with *any* branch of learning and directed to question of the grounds for acceptance of findings in this subject as correct, the methods by which the contents of it are to be attested, and the answer to be given in case one asks about what this science tells us, "But how do you know that?" In physics, for example, over and above all the books devoted to presentation of physical facts and physical laws, there are such studies as Bridgman's *The Logic of Modern Physics*, Lenzen's *The Nature of Physical Theory*, and Margenau's *The Nature of Physical Reality*. In mathematics, over and above all the books presenting the contents of various branches of mathematics, we have such works as Dedekind's famous monograph *Was sind und was sollen die Zahlen?*, Hilbert's *Foundations of Geometry*, and Whitehead and Russell's *Principia Mathematica*. This last, for example, would hardly be celebrated for any signal contribution to the *contents* of mathematics, since there are 378 pages of it before it arrives at the proof that $1 + 1 = 2$; but it stands as a landmark in the *theory* of mathematics by establishing that we know that mathematics is true if logic is true, because the theorems of mathematics are derivable from paradigms of logic together with definitions of the mathematical concepts in terms of those of logic. In other words it is addressed to the question "How do you know what you know in mathematics? What is the foundation of mathematical truth?" There are similar theories-of correlative with any other branch of science, usually written by masters of the science in question and directed to questions of the methods by which investigations in this subject are validly to be pursued, the criteria by which validity of results are to be attested, and the valid interpretation to be put upon such established results. And if there is any further topic sure to be discussed in any such theory-of, it will be the significance of the basic *concepts* involved in the science it deals with—precisely what this science applies to.

It is important to note that when one is concerned, say in physics, with questions of the theory of physics—for example, "How do you know physical truths?", "How do you attest physical findings?", "How is the significance of physical laws to be correctly interpreted?"—one cannot use the methods of physics, or appeal to physical findings, for the discovery and corroboration of any answer which can be given to them. Instead one must appeal to critical reflection, and if there is any branch of study which might be pertinent to such critical investigations comprised in any theory-of, it would be logic and epistemology. "How do you know X?" and "How do you establish the correctness of a finding, X?" are always such logico-epistemological questions, regardless of what the subject matter—X—is. If, in view of the necessity for analyzing basic concepts, something further might be called for, that could be metaphysics. As Einstein said, "I believe that every true physicist is a kind of tamed metaphysicist."* This should not surprise us: the theory of any branch of knowledge is simply the critical assessment of it *as* a branch of *knowledge*. What is pertinent to that assessment may depend in part on the kind of knowledge it is, or claims to be: on whether, for example, it is supposedly *a priori* knowledge, like mathematics and logic, or is empirical knowledge, like any of the natural sciences. But for the rest and mainly, it will be the same general type of examination which is called for in any theory-of, and directed

* Albert Einstein, "On the Generalized Theory of Gravitation," *Scientific American*, Vol. 182, No. 4 (April 1950), p. 13.

to the same kind of question: the certification of this branch of learning as a valid cognitive procedure, capable of yielding cognitively valid results.

All this may seem a bit aside from our problem of the foundations of ethics. It is, however, relevant in two respects, both fundamental for our project. First, it indicates that this question of the validity of ethical principles, in general and in particular, is the same kind of question—even if it should not admit of the same kind of answers—which may arise with reference to any other branch of study if the findings of it should be challenged. In ethics, it is the question how we can determine and assure—or *whether* we can determine and assure—what we must claim to know when we declare that anything is right, or is wrong, to do, or when we set up or accept any principle of ethics, or any body of such principles, as valid directives of our conduct.

And second, these considerations which point to the locus of this question of the validity of ethics as lying in the logical significance of our ethical concepts, and the epistemological—and possibly metaphysical—character of our ethical findings, may serve to orient us better to the present scene so far as ethics is concerned. What we are witnessing, in present-day challenges to the objective validity of ethics, is a revival of the sophistic doubts—an immensely more sophisticated formulation of these doubts, to be sure, and much more meticulously and circumspectly explored, but fundamentally having the same import, nevertheless, as those which were pressed in the fifth century B.C. The doubt is that any statement to the effect that so-and-so is right, or is wrong, is demonstrably correct, true; that there is any matter of ascertainable fact to be so expressed; that any such conviction could represent knowledge of any kind. Ethical statements and moral convictions are being challenged by the allegation that they are noncognitive. It is being said that they are merely relative to the particular culture which exhibits them, or that they are merely expressions of emotive attitudes of approval and disapproval, in contrast to any matter of determinable fact. Somewhat curiously, however, those who presently revive such doubts of the moral validities omit to extend their doubts, as the ancient sophists did, to knowledge at large. And they likewise appear not to discover any relevant lesson in the wider skepticism of Hume; though if they have discovered any new and decisive answer to Hume's skepticism, I do not know what it is or where they have set it forth. But in contrast to Hume, our contemporary skeptics of the moral often couple a positivistic emphasis upon the validity of science with their negativistic attitude toward ethics.

Most frequently, they also extend their skeptical doubt beyond ethics and the moral to include the valuational, and hence to the normative at large. In that, I think they are at least consistent: the moral and the valuational go together, and there hardly could be any foundation for valid moral principles and assessments of the right and wrong in general without some like ground for valid judgments of the good and bad. Indeed, as will appear hereafter, I think that any defense of moral judgment as possibly objective and having cognitive significance must depend upon a similar defense of appraisals of the good and bad as likewise cognitive in significance and addressed to a certain kind of determinable fact.

It is a grim coincidence that this current attack upon the validity of the moral and the valuational should come in just the period when the moral core of Western civilization falls under the most severe challenge it has ever had to meet. Though it has no weight as argument, this present juncture in world affairs must have its weight as pointing up the seriousness of this issue concerning the bases of moral judgment. If there is no manner of demonstrable fact, and no appeal to the common rationality of men, by which it could be determined what is right and justified to do, and what is wrong and unjustified to do, then there could be no decisive ground whatever on which such conflicts of attitude and of conviction can be resolved—except by that last arbitrament which is always open when all else fails, the arbitrament of force. Indeed that is the very core of the issue—somewhat amazingly, a metaphysical issue—whether the destiny of man is amenable to his sense of what is good and what is right or is instead something cosmically written as the inevitable outcome of a dialectic of history dominated by the material needs and clashes of the creature who is what he eats (*ist was er isst,* Feuerbach). It is a curious and dreadful fact that just at the time when science has put into the hands of men the most powerful instruments for control of their environment—ambivalently capable of use for human betterment or for the suicide of civilization—we should be told, by some of those who celebrate science as the outstanding triumph of the human mind, that appraisals of the good and bad and assessments of the right and wrong have nothing more fundamental as their basis and their sanction than our emotive drives and our subjective persuasions of attitude.

If this issue is a philosophical one—and I am afraid it is—then it is time that our philosophy should catch up with our science. Otherwise it seems possible that the products of science, instead of yielding the manifold and immense benefits which they are capable of conferring on us, might lead to destruction of the civilization which has produced this scientific triumph, and this power for control of our human future.

The Right and the Good

We have so far been principally engaged with the difference between questions *in* Ethics, "What is it morally right to do in this case, or this kind of case?", to which an accepted moral precept may give the answer; and questions which belong to the Theory of Ethics, "Whatever it is which is morally right to do, what makes it so?", which concerns the validity of precepts, the foundations of the morally right.

If one ask "What ought I to do in this instance, or under these circumstances?", it will be sufficient to cite a moral precept one accepts as valid covering the point: for example, "You ought to pay this money you owe because debts ought always to be paid." And if one ask the further question, "But *why* should debts always be paid?", or "*Should* debts always be paid?", it may still be possible to answer by reference to moral principles, because there may be a higher and more general precept from which the one first cited follows: for example, "Debts should always be paid because incurring a debt is implicitly a promise to pay, and promises made should be kept." But if the questioner be persistent enough, or perverse enough, then he can repeat his question "Why?", this time about promise-keeping, and eventually a different kind of answer must be found—one which will not be itself a precept of ethics but assign some ground on which ethical pronouncements can be assured as valid. And the question of this ground of assurance, or test of validity in ethics, is not itself a question *in* ethics but one concerning the *foundations* of ethics. The same thing would be true if the question concerned a law of physics, or of any other science, instead of a law of morals—a precept of ethics. The question "What will assure that a generalization in the language of physics is truly a law of physics and to be accepted as valid?" is not a question to be answered *finally* by citing other and more general laws of physics, but one concerning the grounds of that branch of study called physics—the grounds on which a statement is to be accepted as physical truth—and that question belongs, not to physics, but to Theory of Physics.

Moral rightness is not the only kind of rightness to be inquired about. But if it should be some other species of the right which is in question—for example, the legally right, or the artistically right, or the medically right—the situation would be fundamentally the same: there would be formulatable precepts of the kind of practice in question, which would give the answer to the first question, whether a particular act under consideration would or would not be right to do; but there would also be this second question of the ground on which *directives* of this species of practice are to be attested as valid and right *directives*. And as in morals, so also in artistic practice: for example, the question what it will be artistically right to do may in the first instance be answered by citing a precept of pictorial art, such as a principle of composition or the principle of perspective. But if the questioner be persistent and ask "But *why* should pictures be so composed?", or "*Is* it imperative to conform one's drawing to the principle of perspective?", then this second question is not one to be answered by citing other directives of artistic practice, but must be answered eventually by a theory of aesthetics, which concerns the foundation of valid principles of art themselves.

There may be—indeed there must be—something which is specific to and distinctive of the morally right, or the aesthetically right, or any other species of our doing which there is some reason to set off and consider by itself. And principles of one such kind of right practice may well reflect some difference in the ground and criteria of this particular category of practice. But presumably there will be also something which is common to rightness in all these diverse species of it—some common mark of the difference between right doing and wrong doing in all these different kinds of cases, and wherever this distinction of right and wrong is made. Otherwise the use of the same words, 'right' and 'wrong', would have no explanation, or else must be merely a metaphorical or oblique use of language in every kind of case but one—and that is not plausible. And whatever this common meaning of 'right' and 'wrong' should be, it must indicate some common feature which distinguishes the right from the wrong in all these various species of it; and is, thus, what "makes right right," wherever you find it.

It might be well to begin with this question of the ground on which whatever is right to do in any sense is attestable as being such, leaving the further question of the morally right and what is peculiar to it as one species to be considered later. Especially this may be judicious if we have in mind the challenge of that skepticism mentioned in the preceding lecture, because these doubts raised concerning the validity of moral principles most frequently turn upon questions regarding right and wrong in general rather than upon anything which is peculiar to the moral. Their being directed against principles of the *morally* right in particular seems most often to reflect nothing in the *arguments* put forward. Indeed their being so directed against the validity of moral directives, to the neglect of the parallel directives of artistic or medical and other kinds of practice, might arouse some suspicion of initial bias, and at least must stand as a major oversight on the part of these critics of the moral validities.

Looking to the right and wrong in general, and to the question "Why ought one to do so-and-so?", without regard to what manner of ought it is which is in point, common sense has a frequent way of meeting this query or this challenge which is at least suggestive of the direction in which we might look if we wish to find out on what ground it is that whatever is called right is determined to be such. When a child or an inexperienced person raises this troublesome question why he ought to do, or to refrain from doing, as we advise, we sometimes answer impatiently, "Well, go ahead and do as you please, and you will find out why." The suggestion is, of course, that acts have consequences which will be found gratifying or disconcerting when they are later realized. And giving such an answer indicates that desirable and undesirable consequences play an essential part in determining what acts ought and what ought not to be done. The same thing is suggested also by the manner in which we sometimes challenge a proposed course of conduct, asking "But *what good* would that do?"

There are sound reasons why we could not accept this suggestion that we can, in all cases, determine whether an act is right to do or not *simply* by looking to the good or bad consequences of it. But we shall certainly be on the side of common sense if we think that at least there could be no settling of this question whether an act is right or is wrong to do *without* consideration of the good or bad results of acting in that way.

If it were not for the fact that some things gratify and some things grieve, nobody would have any concern over what he, or anybody else, should bring about. If there were no such fact as good and bad in the experience of life, there would also be no such fact as right and wrong in what is done. Nobody would have any reason to care.

In a world in which there should be no conscious experience of the good and bad, directives of action would have no significance and no validity, because actions themselves would be pointless. In such a world, whatever happened or failed to happen, nobody would be concerned or have a preference. And if, observing this essential connection between right and wrong on the one side, and good and bad on the other, one should ask, "But which comes first, good and bad or right and wrong?", the answer is clearly evident. There *could* be a world in which conscious beings enjoyed and suffered but without their marking any distinction between the right and wrong to do: *this* world was like that in the age of the dinosaurs and before the arrival of animals endowed with intelligence. But there could not be any distinction of right and wrong for intelligent beings to make in a world in which they should experience nothing as being good or bad. It is the sense of good and bad which is primal, and the sense of right and wrong to do which is derivative and dependent. Perhaps we can add to this, as a matter of common sense, that if it should be clear that an act could not possibly bring any grief or harm to anyone, there could be no sense in calling it wrong to do; and if it should be clear that an act could not possibly bring anything but grief or harm to anyone affected by it, then it would be outrageous to call it right to do. There have been a few moralists who would not agree to this; but perhaps that itself is enough to render their moral theory suspect.

Ethics has, of course, always taken cognizance of an essential connection between the right and the good, the wrong and the bad; and there never has been any full-bodied theory of ethics which has not included some conception of the *summum bonum* and the ideally good life. But our particular interest here is in the possibility that the question how it is to be determined what directives of our doing are correct and valid can be given a partial answer at least: namely, "Only such directives of our doing can be valid as direct us to do what is sanctioned by some reliability of its leading to good results." That, again, might appear to be, out of hand, just common sense. And while it may be the case that what is just common sense is oftentimes not good enough, it would be highly unfortunate, as well as a little implausible, that the general business of our self-government, which no individual can finally resign to any other, is a matter beyond the purview of the common man. What fails of accord with common sense must have, in morals at least, a presumption against it. And we may even say: "Find out what precepts of action, if generally heeded by all of us in common, would guarantee the continual betterment of human life, and we will incorporate them in our ethics."

The same simple suggestion will have its pertinence to problems of the right in every sense of right: a precept of the right must, in order to be valid, be a reliable recipe for achieving good results—or better results than we should know how to achieve in any other way. Finding out such recipes and how to follow them is, of course, the practically hard part of every practical problem. That is where the arts and special sciences come in—including that art we must all aspire to command, the art of the good life. But I think we may safely take as a common mark of what is right doing, in any sense of right, that it must represent a way of doing which experience has attested as reliably leading to good results, and accept it as a test of any valid precept of the right at large that it must be a directive formulating such a way of acting. The *desideratum* of all activity is to achieve something desirable: that is a tautology. And no way of acting which does not satisfy that requirement could be right. The best-judged objection to this conception of the outstanding criterion of the right at large would be to say that it is a commonplace, and that to elevate this commonplace to the position of a theoretic determinant of the right is merely a pedantic gesture. As already indicated, I should be happy to plead guilty to this indictment—barring adjectives. I take it that philosophers have nothing to tell people which they do not already know, or will not be prepared to accept after they have thought the matter through; and the worst fault any philosophy could commit would be to overlook or fail of accord with what is obvious.

In any case, however, this *sine qua non* of the right at large will not be sufficient to validate the precepts of the right in its more specific senses—the technically right, the prudentially right, or the morally right. That also lies in the nature of the case, and—if it should need any corroboration—is immediately made evident by the fact that what is right in one of these senses may be wrong in another. In order that we may have in mind the most essential point needing further consideration, let us state that general point at once. It is a *necessary* condition of the rightness of an act, and of the validity of any directive of doing, that the way of acting in question be one we are justified in expecting to lead to a good result. But this is not always a *sufficient* condition of the rightness of an act or the validity of a directive of action.

The necessary condition of assurance of a good result comes

27

nearest to being also a sufficient condition in the case of the technically right, and we may proceed to that at once. As previously illustrated, it is a distinctive feature of judgments of the technically right that they concern the manner in which we should best proceed in order to achieve a certain kind of end, but they include no critique of that end itself, simply assuming that this end in question will sometimes be one it is justified to pursue. They are, so to say, judgments of how to accomplish rather than directives of what we should or should not address ourselves to bringing about in any given case. Characteristically, technical rightness also concerns routines of practice directed to some specific purpose, or class of related purposes, calling for some particular manner of expertness, such as that of some craft or profession. The general need for such craftsmanship or professional know-how may be taken for granted. It is because of such need that the expertness in question has been socially approved and fostered. There is good food to be produced and cooked, good houses to be built, good music to be made; and always there will be cases in which good health will need to be restored.

But as already suggested, judgment of any act as technically right is never a final judgment of that act as right to do. An occasion in question may be one on which the aim of a particular technique may be a wrong end to pursue; and any technique may be so misapplied. Also there are those exceptional kinds of skill the exercise of which will, more often than not, contravene social purposes and be a wrong thing to do. There is a right way to blow a safe, a right way to open doors without the key, and a right way to make counterfeit ten dollar bills. But the fact that the safe was blown in just the right way to accomplish that purpose, or the counterfeit bill was made with the utmost skill, will not save the practitioner's act from general condemnation.

Every deliberate act has some end in view to which it is directed. And every act may be judged with reference to this proximate purpose of it—judged as well or ill taken merely for the attainment of that purpose. The assessment of technical rightness is such a judgment. Characteristically, however, the end in view when the word 'technique' applies will be something thought of as good in the sense of 'good for', and desirable because it is a means to something further, rather than being desirable for its own sake and as an end in itself. And even where, as in the physician's practice, the end in view is also an end in itself, judgment of the action taken as technically right does not have direct reference to the relation of this act to this intrinsically desirable end but rather to some more specific and more immediate purpose contributory to that end —improvement of the patient's digestion, for example, or production of more red corpuscles or of specific antibodies.

However, the *reason why* the assessment of technical rightness is never a final assessment of the act as right is not that the determination of acts as right or wrong requires to be made, or even can be made, by reference to any other criterion than the goodness or badness of the predictable consequences of the act in question. Instead, it is because there are *different senses* of 'good', just as there are different senses of 'right'; and assessment of the act as technically right turns on appraisal of its consequences as *instrumentally* good—"good for" something else. In contrast, the assessment of an act as finally right or completely right must turn upon appraisal of its consequences as good in an equally final sense—the sense of 'good in itself' or 'good for its own sake'. Technical rightness is a subordinate and nonfinal sense of 'right' because the correlative sense of 'good'—'instrumentally good'—is a subordinate and nonfinal sense of 'good'. It is principally for the sake of drawing our attention to this relation between right, in the different senses of that word, and correlative different senses in which good and bad are ascribed, that so long a discussion of the technically right has been inserted here.

We must return, at a later point, to further consideration of the different senses of 'good' so suggested. But without reference to that, there are two other and more general considerations which, taken together, reinforce the conclusion that no judgment of right or wrong can validly be made except by reference to appraisal of predictable consequences of the act in question as good or bad. First, no act has any content, by reference to which it can be indicated as the act spoken of, except *consequences* of the initiation of it, actual or expected. If I am asked what I am doing, there is no answer I can make except by reciting consequences I expect to bring about, or am trying to bring about. The act is done—committed—when the initiative of willing it is taken, and before any consequences appear; but I can tell anyone else, or even tell myself, what act it is that I so commit myself to, only by some recital of what this commitment is to bring about. Other than that, this act has no intelligible content. And—the second point—as we have already observed, the only consequences of anything which could have any importance for anyone and concern him to bring about, or to avoid, or to have others bring about or avoid, must be consequences which, in some sense and to somebody, are either good or bad. Neither the prudentially right nor the morally right could turn upon any other and essentially different kind of consideration.

The strongly suggested conclusion is that without reference

to what is good and what is bad there could be no determination of anything as right or wrong to do—to bring about. But *if* it is known, or can be found out, what acts lead to good results and what to bad, then the way is open for determination of the rightness or wrongness of the act which produces these effects. Without knowledge of the good and bad there can be no knowledge of the right and wrong; but *with* knowledge of the good and bad there may also be knowledge of what it is right and what it is wrong to do.

The importance of clarity on this point lies in the bearing of it on the question whether what is right and what is wrong represent a certain kind of *facts* which can be found out—whether or not determinations of right and wrong represent a kind of possible *knowledge*. It is precisely this which our contemporary skeptics of the moral validities would put in doubt. They do not, like the ancient sophists and like Hume, doubt that there are any determinable nonanalytic facts of which we can have knowledge, but they doubt that determinations of the right and wrong are amongst such cognitively discoverable facts. They might also accept our conclusion, above, that *if* we can know what is good and what is bad, we can, from that, also determine what is right and what is wrong: it is difficult to say because they seldom consider that question explicitly. But whatever they might admit on just that point, they would still maintain that it does not prove that assessments of the right and wrong are determinations of any kind of matter of fact. Their doubt in this matter would persist because they would, in any case, deny that *appraisals of the good and bad* represent any kind of knowledge of determinable matters of fact. While perhaps admitting that there is some kind of distinction between assessments of the right and wrong and appraisals of the good and bad—that point is not, for them, of fundamental importance—they characteristically lump the two together, and refuse to accept either one of them as representing a kind of knowledge. Thus, if we entertain any hope that we can meet their skeptical doubts and show their position untenable, we shall have to pursue this issue into the area where it concerns valuations—appraisals of the good and bad.

I hope it will be apparent to you that I do not invent this complication of the matter. I take it as I find it; and we shall have to follow the argument wherever it may lead. But I would pause upon this point, not presently to argue—the argument will come later—but to emphasize, because we now come to the crux of this whole matter of the defense of —literally—everything that we hold dear. To hold dear, to set high, to take to be of worth and importance—do such attitudes have objective significance and justification; or are they, at bottom, merely subjective and baseless? The good and the right stand for the final motivations of any life which cherishes its own aims as significant and takes that to which it is devoted to have a character justifying such devotion. Are these motivations merely postures that we strike, and of no real import, because there is no kind of fact at all to which they answer? That is the question.

I point out so far that this question, as applied to the right and wrong, seems to depend on the similar question about the good and bad—about values—because the validity of the distinction between right and wrong, which concerns our decisions and deliberate doings, depends on the antecedent distinction between good and bad in that which our deciding and doing may bring about. Thus we are obliged to consider first the question of this prior and correlative distinction between the good and bad, and the question of the cognitive character of our valuations.

Valuations and judgments of the right and wrong are customarily bracketed together and marked off from other types of judgment by being called normative: there are norms—standards—of the right, and there are also standards of value. Also, normative judgments of both kinds are frequently spoken of as valuations, and what they judge of are often called values. However, this verbal lumping together of the good and the right, under the one word 'values', is highly unfortunate. The distinction of them is as important as their similarity and the connection of them, and much confusion in ethical theory is due to the failure to mark them off from one another. Basically that distinction is simple: 'right' and 'wrong' apply to our decisions and our deliberate doing; 'good' and 'bad' apply to all sorts of things—almost anything you can think of—and are not confined to what may be a consequence of action and need to be considered in deciding what to do.

If we could say simply, "Right acts are those which lead to good results; wrong acts are those which lead to bad ones," then the rest of the matter might also be quite simple. And is not that just what I have said? No: if that has been suggested to you, I will not disclaim responsibility for allowing this suggestion, but as a matter of fact I have been quite careful *not* to say just that. That would be a good rough first approximation, and I have indeed tried to begin with the simplicities of the matter. But we now arrive at the point where we shall have to deal with some of the complexities.

A first complexity arises from the fact that, for a very important reason, we judge somewhat differently when the

question is "Right or wrong?" than when it is "Good or bad?"
It will be a clear illustration of the point if we return to the
example used before, of choosing an investment. (And let us
remember that this will be a question of prudentially right
doing if it should be my own money to be invested, a question
of morally right doing if it is the money of another for whom
I am trustee.) Suppose I weigh the alternatives of investing
in stock A, in bond B, or in a piece of real estate C. On all the
evidence I can muster, bond B looks most promising, and I
decide on that. But six months later, bond B shows a consider-
able loss in market value, whereas stock A has gone away up
in price, and I have just learned that oil has been discovered
on the parcel of real estate C which I decided against. Things
like that happen, you know: life is that way. Nobody can
foresee completely and with certainty the consequences of any
act he may choose to do. But he has to decide.

Shall I say, in this case, that I made a *good* investment?
No, that announcement would now be laughable: a *good*
investment is one that turns out well, one that *proves* to be
good, whether that result is due to wise foresight or merely
to good luck. But was it a *right* investment for me to make;
or did I do wrong, and should I blame myself now for having
made it? If the answer is less than perfectly clear in this case,
that may be because we often fail of perfect precision in the
use of the words in question, often saying 'good' when it
would be more accurate to say 'right', and saying 'right' when
'good' would be more exact. But I think the correct answer
will be obvious in this example: the investment will be good
or bad according to the way it turns out—the actual consequences of making it. But the rightness or wrongness of the
act of making it does not depend directly upon this actual
goodness or badness of its consequences: instead, it depends

upon the *justified belief* as to such good or bad consequences on the part of the doer at the time and in the circumstances when he had to make his decision and choose his action. If my best judgment of the consequences of so investing was that it would turn out badly, then obviously I am to blame for this result, and my act was wrong. Also, if I carelessly omitted to weigh the evidence I had, or to get pertinent evidence available, then I am at least partly to blame, and my action could not be said to be unqualifiedly right. But if I acted in accordance with an expectation of good consequences which was justified on all the evidence available to me at the time, then I did all that the angels could do, in those premises of action, and — unqualifiedly — my act was right, however badly it may turn out. And what we may observe in this example holds generally.

Let us sum this matter up. The consequences of an act will be good or bad; but in and of themselves, as events simply, they are neither right nor wrong. They may be said to be right or wrong *to bring about—to do*—but in that case it is the *doing*, the *bringing about*, to which the rightness or wrongness is ascribed. And the doing will be either right or wrong; but we should be careful not to call an action good when what we mean is that it is right. And insofar as we could claim that the rightness of doing depends on the goodness of the consequences, the *most* that we can judiciously claim is that an act is right if it accords with a cogent and justified belief, on evidence available to the doer at the time he had to decide, that the consequences would be good, or at least more good than bad.

However, we are not yet out of the woods—by quite a lot. There are other ways in which 'right' and 'wrong', as applied to acts, could be used; indeed, there is one such other way of using them which is so frequent that it must be accounted good linguistic usage, and—unfortunately, I think—there is at least one theory of ethics based upon this different but linguistically sanctioned usage. For this reason, let us survey, as briefly as possible, three different meanings which conceivably could attach to 'right' as applied to acts. First, we might call an act right just in case its consequences *are* good—or more good than bad, or such as represent that alternative which turns out best. That is, we could class an act as right if and only if it is such as would have been right to choose if the doer's foresight had been *omniscient*. We might label what would be right in this sense 'absolutely right', or speak of the *absolute rightness* of it. As you will now observe, it is in this sense only that it would be correct to say that an act is right to do if and only if the consequences of it *are* good. But since nobody has or can have such omniscient foresight of the consequences of acts, it is only the historian—and certainly not the moralist—who could apply 'right' in this sense of absolutely right. This usage hardly needs to be mentioned in ethics except in order to eliminate it. However, let us note in passing that such absolute rightness represents a sort of ideal—just as absolute truth represents an ideal. In fact, those two go together: precisely the reason why what it is *humanly* right to do does not coincide with the absolutely right is that our human foresight must fall short of absolute assurance and absolute truth. And, both in our deliberate doing and in our deliberated beliefs, we seek to come as close as we can to this ideal of the absolute.

The second sense of 'right' as applied to acts is that which we have already outlined in discussing our example of investing money. Let us call that the *objective rightness* of an action. An act is objectively right if, on all the data open to him when he must decide, the doer believes that the consequences of it will be good, or better than any alternative, *and* this expectation is a *justified* belief. Since, as we have just seen, such a belief could not be assured with theoretic certainty, it comes to the same thing to say that an act is objectively right if and only if, on the available evidence, it is genuinely *probable* that its consequences will be good, or better than those of any alternative. Let me explain the significance of 'objective' in 'objectively right'. Anything is objective if it is as it is regardless of what anybody thinks about it. And let us note that the probability of anything, on a given body of data, *is* just what it is and not otherwise, regardless of what anybody thinks. Also this probability on any specified body of data remains just what it is even if, on some *other* or some *larger* body of data, there would be a different probability of the same thing. And it is in accord with this that an act which is objectively right, and which, on the data open to the doer at the time when he did it, will probably have good results, remains an act it was objectively right for him to do, no matter how it turns out and whether the actual results prove to be good or not. It should also be noted that the objective rightness of an act requires that this probability of good results be *correctly determined* from its data; to be objectively right the doer's prediction of good results must be one which is cogently made. We hold ourselves responsible for straight thinking about probable results, as well as for good intentions, in what we do deliberately.

It is rightness in this second sense of the objectively right to do that it is mainly important to consider in ethics. But there is still a third sense which we could not omit from consideration: the sense in which an act is right if the doer's *intentions* in doing it are good (right) intentions, regardless of

37

any further consideration. This we may call the *subjective rightness* of an act. To determine what it is objectively right to do, we must not only utilize properly all the relevant evidence open to us in forecasting the probable consequences of the doing, but we must also utilize it *cogently*. And all of us are capable of negligence in observing relevant evidence open to us in forecasting what may happen in consequence of an act, as well as liable to stupidity on occasion and to *incogency* in such prediction. And even if we blame ourselves whenever we find that we have been thus negligent or stupid, we can hardly blame others, unqualifiedly, for such negligence or stupid failure to be cogent. Whatever is, by reason of such negligence or incogency, overlooked or not foreseen correctly, is *not intended*; our intentions in doing are confined to what we *expect* as result of the act. And an act is subjectively right if it is done with the *intention* to bring about good results.

To sum up, then, an act is *absolutely* right if its consequences are cogently expected to be good and *are* good; it is *objectively* right if they are *cogently expected* to be good, whether they actually are good or not; and it is *subjectively* right if they are expected to be good, whether this expectation is cogent or not.

The particular reason why we need this third sense of right —subjective rightness—in addition to that of objective rightness is that we have two different problems concerning right doing, neither of them avoidable. First, we have to decide what it will be right for us to do—not absolutely right, but as near to that as human foresight and cogency allow. Objective rightness answers that question. But second, we also have to judge whether to blame, and perhaps punish, or to praise, and perhaps reward, other people for what they deliberately do. And we do not blame others, or punish them, for what is due merely to their stupidity and is unintentional. If, contrary to their expectation and intention, they bring about results which are bad, we may point out to them that what they did was a wrong thing to choose to do; but this wrongness is in their *thinking,* not in that which they foresightedly and deliberately committed themselves to bring about. And why do we need this category of the subjectively right? We need it because *we* are responsible for our own praising and blaming, rewarding and punishing; and the ground of *just* praising and blaming is the subjective—intended—rightness or wrongness of the doing.

In conclusion, let us return to consideration of our position —so far—*vis-à-vis* that of one who is skeptical of the moral validities. We have now observed that any deliberate doing involves prediction of consequences: predicted consequences of our willed initiative are what we say we do. That an act is subjectively right does not indeed require valid knowledge, but it does require a cognitive conviction—an expectation of certain consequences. The point of subjectivity about it is that it does not require that this conviction be true or even cogent and valid. But to call even such a subjective determination of the right to do noncognitive is incorrect. Even false predictions are cognitive, and without prediction of its consequences no deliberate act could even be done at all.

Objective rightness requires not only the prediction of consequences but requires also that these predictions be cognitively valid—requires that they be cogent predictions on the basis of the evidence open to the doer. And that is the same as requiring that these foreseen consequences be genuinely probable on the evidence available when the decision of action has to be taken by the doer.

However, these considerations do not fully disprove the

skeptic's contention. They fail to do so because he can fall back on his further contention that goodness and badness are not knowable or demonstrable properties of anything. And—we admit—it is the goodness or badness of the consequences of deliberate acts which must be knowable in order to determine whether an act is right or wrong. We must, therefore, in order to make good our case against the skeptic, consider his contention that *valuations* are not cognitive determinations of any objective property of the thing called good or bad. The question whether ascriptions of value to a thing represent cognitive determination of a character of this thing which is as it is and not otherwise, regardless of what is thought about it—that must be our next topic.

Doubts About Ethics

This too brief series of lectures is mainly directed to an attempt to answer the skeptic who says that our moral convictions are without foundation because there are no objective facts for them to rest on and by reference to which the correctness of them can be attested. The best way to meet an objector who says that there isn't any such thing as X—whatever X may be—is to show him an X: the best way to meet one who doubts that there is any foundation for moral judgments is to show him what the basis of them is. That is the egregious task which I undertake to outline here.

However, I shall someday, I feel sure, be accused of approaching this matter of the foundations by going around Robin Hood's barn: by discussing, first, the right in general— whether it be the morally right, the prudentially right, the logically right, or right in any other sense—and then looking to the good in general, and in its various senses, as the justifying aim of whatever it is right to do. My excuse for this roundabout approach must be that those who attempt any more direct one fail to arrive—or at least to convince me that they arrive—at their intended destination. I fear that there is no shorter cut to understanding the grounds of valid moral judgment.

Supposing that, in general, what it is right to do is so because of some good which it may achieve, we observed that there is nevertheless an important difference between the way in which we judge of what is good and the manner in which we determine the rightness of what we do. When we say that a thing is good, we do *not* mean merely that we *suppose* it good: we mean that it *is* good, that it will *prove* to be good, that the goodness of it can be *attested*. But granting that the rightness of acts has essential reference to the goodness of their consequences, still it is necessary to observe that when we say an act is *right* we do *not* mean that the consequences of it will *prove* to be good. At *most* what we mean is that, in the circumstances and at the time when the doer had to decide his action, he *believed* that the consequences of it would be good *and*, on all the evidence then available to him, that belief was cogent and justified. An act so decided is *objectively* right. And the *least* that we could well mean by saying that an act is right is that the doer expected—believed—that the consequences would be good, whether that belief was cogent and justified or not. An act which thus springs from good intentions—expectations of doing good—is *subjectively* right.

If this distinction between the objectively right and that which is merely subjectively right proves troublesome, let us think of bidding at bridge. One has the evidence of his own hand and of whatever is to be inferred from bids the others may have made. From that, one has to forecast the probable results if he or his partner should be called upon to play out the hand and make good his bid. If he correctly estimates the probable results on the basis of the evidence he has, and bids accordingly, then he has made the *objectively* right bid, no matter how the play actually turns out. If he fails to make this objectively right choice, perhaps his partner will afterwards instruct him as to the bid he should have made. In that case, he can only console himself with the thought that at least he did his stupid best; and his bid, though not in accord with the probabilities on the evidence he should have noted, was innocently made and *subjectively* right. His intentions were perfect. (Incidentally, I never play bridge.)

It is objective rightness which is the major question of ethics, because that is the question whose answer one who asks what it will be right to do is seeking to find out: what act which he may choose has best assurance of good results. If it were a question of his own good *intentions* only, he would hardly need to ask. The goodness of the results is that matter of fact which he must weigh. At the time when we must decide action, we can never be certain about that kind of fact, but we can think cogently about it—barring some ungetoverable stupidity. And this is the same as to say that we can correctly weigh the probability affecting it, on all the evidence available to us. If we so determine cogently the probable goodness or badness of the alternatives open to us, and conform our action to what offers the best assurance of good results, we shall be doing the best that it is humanly possible to do; and to say that we did wrong, if or when it turns out badly, would make no sense—or at least, not that kind of sense we are concerned about in making moral judgments.

We should also remark in passing that the fact that predictions of the consequences of actions are, theoretically, no better than probable is not a good reason for refusing to call them knowledge. In the field of what has to be learned from experience, *no* knowledge can be, theoretically, better than probable. Though it is too commonly overlooked, that is the only sense in which what any natural science tells us can be called knowledge—the sense of being cogently determined probabilities about some class of future observable events, on the basis of all the evidence up to now. Of course, many of these theoretical probabilities are so high as to be what we appropriately call practical certainties. But that is as true in morals as it is in physics. It is practically certain that poking somebody in the eye with a picket stick will not do him any good (the theoretical possibility that the poke might cause him to jump back just in time to escape a bullet and save his life being practically negligible). On this point that it must deal with predictions which are theoretically no better than probable, ethics is no worse off than physics. Unless there is some *other* objection than that to be made, ethics may represent a type of knowledge if physics and the other natural sciences do.

However, we still do not touch the critical objection which the skeptic of the moral validities will be sure to make, because, as we have already observed in the previous lecture, he will not allow our comparison of such judgments as "X is good" with judgments like "X is red" or "X is two feet long," or in general, judgments of those properties which natural science deals with. He will maintain that whether a thing is two feet long is a matter of objective and determinable fact; but he will not agree that whether a thing is good or not is likewise an objective determinable fact, which is as it is and not otherwise, independently of what anyone thinks about it. And presumably he will add that, while there can be a probability of any objective fact on evidence relevant to it, there cannot be even a genuine probability about anything which is not itself an objectively determinable fact.

We must, then, make examination of the comparison between such statements as "X is good" and those like "X is red"

44

and "X is two feet long." In fact, we must do that in any case because, even on cursory observation, it will be evident that "X is good" may have any one of a wide variety of meanings, just as "X is right" has a variety of meanings, the most important of which we have now attempted to suggest. We must observe, for example, that we often say that something is good meaning only that we like it or that it is good for us; and at other times when we use the same language, what we mean is that this thing is generally good: good for all who are affected by it. And the difference between these two ways of appraising things is correlative with the difference between the aim of prudential doing—our own good—and that of morally right doing—to be adjudged by its effects on all concerned. Again, we sometimes use 'good' in the sense of 'good for', 'good as a means', and at other times in the sense of 'good in itself', 'good for its own sake'. Also it is a complication that there are two major classifications of things to which goodness and badness may be ascribed. First, there are external actualities: objects, events, states of affairs, and the properties of such external realities. And second, there are conscious experiences, and the qualities and characters which experience may have. An object or other external actuality may be good or bad, and an experience may be good or bad; and while most frequently experience of a good object will be a good experience, it is rather often the case that the experience is bad though the object is good, or the experience good though the object is *not* an objectively good thing. The two most important questions to ask about any valuation made are these: first, is it some object or other external actuality whose value is being assessed, or is it a conscious experience whose desirability is being appraised; and second, is this value which is attributed a value which this thing has for

45

its own sake, or a value it has only by reason of conducing to something else and for the sake of something else?

I must pause upon these two questions, because correct account of them is a matter which is fundamental. If we miss the facts here, we are likely to be mistaken throughout. And strangely enough, our commonly used language fails, almost completely, to afford the essential clues to the basically necessary distinctions. Over and above all external actualities, there are *experiences* which are actual. No experience is identically the same thing as any external reality, even though it should be an experience *of* this externally existing thing. And no external existent is identically the same thing as any experience. An experience is actual if and when it occurs. And experiences have qualities and characters which are actual properties of these actually occurring experiences. And no fact about any experience as such is identically the same fact as any fact about external actualities as such.

Perhaps there is nobody who would flatly deny anything of what I have just said; but unfortunately there are some who say things which are totally at variance with what I have just said. There are many nowadays who have a kind of inhibition by reason of which—while they are talking philosophy at least—they seek to avoid discussion of anything directly and simply in terms of experience. But I cannot avoid doing violence to any such inhibition, being convinced that without reference to conscious experience and the characters and qualities which experiences have or may have, there could be nothing in the world which would be either good or bad, and without the distinction of good and bad, there would be nothing to be done which would be either right or wrong. Without the difference between *good experience* and *bad ex-*

perience, there would be no point in valuing anything, and no point in doing anything.

But if these things be so, and you agree, then it follows— does it not?—that there is nothing in the world which is of value strictly for its own sake except experience of that kind and quality such that it is desirable to have experience of that kind, just for the sake of having it. No external reality, nor character or property of one, can be desirable strictly for its own sake. Any object we call good is such because of some character of it by reason of which it is at least capable of bringing about or conducing to some conscious experience—or many such—having the character of good experience, or of conducing to the alleviation of some experience having the character of bad experience.

For the reasons just cited, it is understanding of value-ascriptions as applied to experience which is the first essential for correct understanding of valuation as applied to other things.

Only experiences are desirable strictly for their own sake. But in relation to experience, *objects* may have value in either of two different senses. We must remark the difference between objects which have value by reason of directly gratifying us in the presentation of them—such as a beautiful flower or a work of art—and an object such as a good tool which has value only in the sense of being instrumental to the production or possession of *other objects* having value more directly. Let us here call the value of an object such as the flower or the work of art, which it has by being directly gratifying in the presentation of it, an *inherent* value. And let us call the value of an object which consists in its conducing to the production or possession of some other object, *utility* or *instru-*

mental value. But remembering what we have just said about objects in general, as contrasted with experiences in general, we shall say that *any* value of any object, whether inherent or instrumental, is an extrinsic, not an intrinsic, value of it. No object is good for its own sake and apart from the effect it may have on human life.

We shall also find that *experiences,* and the content of experience, may be good or bad in more than one sense. The most primitive fact which is pertinent here is the fact that experience, as it comes to us, comes with the quality of good or bad. There is a value or disvalue in this quality of good or bad with which it greets us. Perhaps there are also experiences having the quality of the indifferent: better than the definitely bad, not so good as the definitely good. The immediately evident fact is this character of the experience—good, bad, or indifferent—just as we find it to be and not otherwise. (Please note: this value-quality of the experience, just as it comes to us, is a *fact,* a fact with which we are immediately acquainted in having this experience.) I shall call this value-quality, directly found in the experience — the immediate goodness, badness, or indifference of this experience—its *immediate* value or disvalue. And let us note that, with respect to this immediate value of an experience, there is no distinction between appearance and reality. So far as this immediately findable quality of it goes, this experience of it is good if it seems good; and if it seems bad it is bad. The immediate value of an experience is what you immediately find it to be. However, if we attribute the goodness or badness so disclosed to some presented object, the case is then quite different. It could be, for example, a really fine painting which one is looking at, but one might be annoyed by being called away from doing something else to examine it, and find looking at it just now disagreeable. The experience is not gratifying, not immediately good; but the painting may be a good painting, one which we should be happy to have permanently hung on our wall. More often, however, the quality of our experience in viewing the painting would be our best clue to the enduring goodness of the painting—the value of this external object. But in any case, one might do well to defer final judgment of the painting, the decision deciding whether it really is or is not a valuable work of art. But about the immediate goodness or badness of this present experience of looking at it, there is no need for such further judgment; the experienced goodness or badness is just what it seems to be.

But we should observe, however, that such ascription of value or disvalue to experiences—the assessment of them as desirable or undesirable by reason of the immediate quality of them, when and as present—is not the only mode, or even the most important mode, in which we attribute value and disvalue to experiences. We also judge what a particular experience may contribute to some larger whole of experience in which it is ingredient—how much having this experience will add to or detract from the satisfactoriness of our whole vacation, or our whole life. And for a number of reasons, which may be omitted because you will easily find your own examples, an experience which is, within its own temporal boundaries, definitely good in quality may still be such that having it will make life not so good later on. And an experience which is immediately bad, painful even, may still be such that our undergoing it may make life on the whole a better life to live. If students did not realize this fact, some of them would never do much studying. And if professors did not realize it, some of them would not prepare their lectures. Studying or preparing lectures is sometimes not the most gratifying thing one could find to do at the moment. But an academic life in which such ungratifying experiences should not find a place would probably be both short and disagreeable on the whole. Let us call the value or disvalue which an experience may have, *not* by reason of the immediately good or bad quality of it within its own temporal boundaries, but by reason of the influence it exercises upon the quality of experience which comes after, and upon the whole life in which it is included, the *contributory* value of the experience in question.

And now we come to the final and most important point of all concerning value and disvalue as ascribable to experiences as distinct from external objects—important because it may serve to sharpen our understanding of the nature of the problem of the ground of the imperatives of right doing. We have just reviewed two different modes in which value and disvalue are ascribed to experience: value as immediate and value as contributory. And we find that what is correctly denominated good in one of these senses may be correctly denominated bad in the other. They are simply two different modes of the appraisal of experience; and we have to make use of both of them in order to report correctly the facts of life. There is no question of calling one of them the correct way to evaluate experiences and the other incorrect. Each is correct in its own terms; but as appraisals they may be contrary. But which of these two ways of appraising experiences should we look to when the question is that of deciding whether or not to seek, or choose to undergo, or choose to allow ourselves to indulge in a particular experience? To decide according to the value of the experience as immediate, and immediately felt, will be, in general, to follow the dictate of our inclinations; to decide according to the contributory value of the experience will be to follow the dictate of prudence. We say that it is imperative to be prudent. The point is this: if you wish to know *what* it will be prudent to do, the answer to *that* question is to be found by assessing the value of experiences consequent upon any choice of doing to be decided—assessing them according to their contributory value. *What* it is prudentially right to do is a certain kind of fact, intrinsically capable of determination in this manner—though subject to possible error, as all empirical knowledge is. So far as it is the prudentially right which is in question, we here arrive at an answer to the skeptic's challenge "How can you know what it is right to do?", though probably we have not yet met all the objections he will bring against this answer. You know what is prudentially right to do by knowing what choice of action will result in experiences having the greatest contributory value. But we should do well to observe that there is an entirely different question which could be asked here, and which might be thought to be *the* question of the validity of any imperative to follow the dictate of prudence. That is the question "Why should we be prudent?" To *that* question, we have not even attempted yet to offer any clear answer. I think that the moral skeptic, as well as others, sometimes confuses these two questions. He oftenmost does not even raise the question of the validity of prudential dictates, along with the moral, though of course he should in order to be consistent. It is fairly obvious, however, that the situation with regard to the moral will be parallel. The question "Can we know—cognitively determine—what it is morally right to do?" and the question "How do we know that a dictate is a valid moral imperative?" are two quite different kinds of question; and there is no presumption that an argument which should be conclusive with respect to one of them will be even relevant to the other.

Insofar as it is the validity of moral imperatives which the moral skeptic may think to put in doubt, in asserting the non-cognitive character of determinations of the morally right to do, it may be that he is simply off the subject which he supposes himself to be addressing.

I could hardly pass this point without these cautionary observations. But let us now return to the topic of value judgments which this digression interrupted. We have so far said rather little concerning valuations which are addressed, not to experiences and the quality of them, but to objects and the objective value-property of them. The different modes in which value and disvalue are ascribed to objects are more various than those in which they are attributed to experiences. But whatever the more specific meaning of a statement of the form "Object O is a good thing" or "Object O has a certain value," there will be a generic sense which is included in what any such statement will intend, and with respect to which all such value-ascriptions to objects are alike. Any such assertion that an object is good or has a certain positive value will imply that this object has, by its nature, a certain potentiality for contributing to the betterment of some conscious experience. An external existent which could not in any way effect any improvement of the experience of anybody either must be a bad thing, and the existence of it regrettable, or it must be simply worthless, and its existence or nonexistence a matter of rational concern to no one. Objects are good or bad on account of their effects, or possible effects, on conscious life; and apart from that, they have no value or disvalue at all. All objects are good or bad only in the sense of extrinsic value or disvalue—the sense of 'good for' or 'bad for'; and what they are thus good for or bad for is, finally, the quality of some actual or possible experience which they may, directly or indirectly, affect. Apart from its possible effects upon the quality of conscious experience, no object has value or disvalue in any sense at all.

Perhaps so defining the values ascribable to objects—as potentialities for giving rise to experiences having a certain quality—may seem to be a very odd way of conceiving any supposedly objective property of an objective thing, and incomparable to what we mean by saying that an object is red or hard. But if this way of defining the value of an object as a potentiality for conducing to a certain mode of experience seems strange, we might do well to listen to what the physicists are now telling us about these external realities which we may call red or hard or good. These objects really are—so they inform us—whirlpools of electrons, positrons, neutrons, muons, pions, neutrinos, and other particles, the mere list of which presently threatens to exhaust the Greek alphabet. And some of these particles must also be thought of as waves. In our near bewilderment, we would better not ask what, in that case, it is that waves; and let us just forget about antiprotons and other types of antimatter. But if one says that this thing he is looking at is red, it may well seem in point to inquire "What do you mean, 'It is red'?" And should we find anything better to reply than to say that what we mean is that, as a molar mass, this whirlpool of unimaginable what-is-its has a reliable potentiality for inducing the kind of experience called seeing red in a creature endowed with normal human eyes—under appropriate conditions of illumination, of course? Nothing is assertable as true, in physics or any other science, unless it is provable by observation; and let us add that nothing is provable by observation unless by reason of its giving rise directly or indirectly to human experiences of a specific and charaterizable kind, under equally specific and describ-

53

able circumstances. This being so, no scientist can justly claim to have established the objective character of any objective thing unless he should also be able to say, "Tell me the content and character of any experience of observation, and I can tell you whether or not it proves or confirms any scientific statement whose truth I should be competent to judge." Natural scientists seem loath to adopt any such manner of speaking: characteristically they prefer to test the properties of thing A by reference to its effects upon another *thing* B; and this preference for forgetting the observational experience itself is a professional penchant. But can the fact we point out here— the essentiality of specific characteristics of the experience of observation to any specificity of what is so established about what it is an observation *of*—can that be denied? There may be other ways of defining observable properties of things, and there may be good scientific reasons for preferring them, but the possibility and definitive adequacy of delimiting them as potentialities of objects for giving rise to certain specificities of experience cannot well be denied. And there is no basic difference on this point between value-properties and other properties of objects. Or if there is such a difference, it is in favor of value-properties of things, which are much more directly observed than are those which may be ascribed to a meson or a neutrino.

The only further such difference which might be thought important between "It is red" and "It is good" would seem to be that the experience of red is *sensuously* aroused whereas the experience of good is *affective*. But the significance of that distinction could be misconstrued and exaggerated. The affective state conditions what we see, and even more plainly what we do not see, although it is there for our seeing. In general, affection conditions perception, and perception conditions affection. They are almost inseparably conjoined, and the distinction of them is largely an intellectual abstraction in terms of their physiological correlates. For example, is the beauty of a beautiful object sensuously enjoyed or affectively observed? Certainly it is an essential point of the aesthetic experience that in it the affective quality is as directly attributed to the object as is the color or the sound of it. Obviously I cannot, in a brief discussion, do full justice to such points. I must fall back upon the fundamental consideration that the potentiality for conducing to the affective qualifications of experience is as truly a property of the object which *does* induce them as is that kind of property of the object by which it induces the sensory qualifications of experience. It is only a partial cause to be sure, and the antecedent state of the subject may be another; but that is true in both cases, and indeed in all instances where anything can be called a cause of any content of experience aroused by objects. There are always other essential conditions of anything which are not remarked because they can be taken for granted. For example, one cannot see red without the eyes being open, and the character of the object viewed is only a partial cause of the seen redness. Also in both cases the fact of the potentiality belonging to the nature of the object is proved by the fact of the effect.

We may note, however, that we have here the key to the distinction between the inherent values of things, such as the beauty of them, and those values of objects which they have as means and instrumentally only. To be brief about that, the inherent values of objects are sensuously enjoyed in the presence of these objects; the instrumental values are discernible only intellectually, as inferred relationships of cause and effect amongst external things.

Another point about the goodness or badness of objects—

as well as about any other properties ascribable to them as potentialities for conducing to experiences of a certain sort— is that such potentialities are *objective characters of the things* whether the effects they are thus capable of producing are actually realized or not. The saw I bought and hung up in my garage but never seem to find a use for is really a good saw. If I ever *should* need to do some carpenter work, it would cut a board efficiently and with a minimum of effort: those properties are built into it. And the same thing is true of that "gem of purest ray serene the dark unfathom'd caves of ocean bear": if it ever *should* greet human eye, it would glisten and sparkle and would be seen with delight; it *is* objectively that way, in both respects, whatever anybody thinks, and whether these potentialities resident in the nature of it ever actually affect any human experience or not.

The same point that the values of objects are potentialities of them for conducing to value experiences also has its bearing on another distinction in modes of valuation: the distinction between personal value (value to the individual) and social value (value to all concerned). It is a besetting fallacy of value theories to confuse value to persons, which may be different in the case of different persons, with valuations which may be subjective in the sense of invalid. The present point is that valuation in the personal mode may be no more subjective than valuations in the mode of social value. Please remember the meaning of 'subjective' as contrasted with 'objective': that is objective which is as it is and not otherwise, independent of what anybody thinks about it, and is a matter of fact. 'Subjective' has two meanings: a valuation or other judgment is subjective if it is biased, erroneous, not according to the fact; it is also subjective if there is no matter of fact which it addresses, and it could not be either true or false. The

56

skeptic suspects that valuations are subjective in this latter sense, and it may lend plausibility to that suspicion that valuations are frequently personal, *e.g.*, judgments of value to me which would not hold for you. But a judgment of what has value to oneself, though perhaps not to others, may be just as veridical and as much a knowledge of actual fact as a judgment of what is valuable in the impersonal sense. It may be a fact that I need a German-English dictionary whether you do or not; that tennis is good exercise for you but bad for me; that modern music is delightful and listening to it a recreation for you, but a bore and an irritation to me. We humans are quite a lot alike, but each of us is a little different and his circumstances different: what is in fact good for us reflects both our similarities and our differences as well as the similarities and differences of our circumstances.

The confusion of the personal with what is subjective in the sense of nonfactual frequently rests upon another fallacy which besets the arguments of those who deny the cognitive character of value judgments—the fallacy, namely, of confusing the values which things have with the *valuations* which are judgments of them. Or perhaps it will be more just to observe that, since they may be skeptics who deny that there are any objective value facts, the valuations made are, for them, the only pertinent facts to be noted. The value of an object is the good it is capable of doing. That is a kind of testable fact. The valuation of it is somebody's judgment of that fact. Valuations can be as erroneous and are as liable to mistake as judgments of any other kind of fact. Values, by contrast, are what they *prove* to be; and the valuations are either true or not, and either justified beliefs or not. We say to the child, "You think you want that, but you will be disappointed if you get it." One or the other of us is right and one is wrong;

which is which will be found out if or when he gets it. Our adult wantings may likewise prove to be mistakes—mistaken ascriptions of value to the objects of them. Our attitudes of favoring may similarly reflect misjudgments of values: we may favor something unworthy of our favoring, be interested in something which will not satisfy our interest in it. And this very fact that favoring, being interested in, desiring, and other such attitudes can prove to be mistaken proves that the *valuations* they reflect are *judgments of fact*—assessments of something which is as it is and not otherwise, independently of what is thought about it.

Unfortunately, this fallacy of confusing values, which are attestable facts about things, with the valu*ings*, which represent what somebody *thinks* about some such facts, is so common as to have given rise to a second meaning of the word 'value'. For example, if a sociologist heads his monograph "Hopi Values," you may be quite sure he is *not* going to discuss what is good for the Hopi people: he would regard that as unprofessional. What his monograph will be devoted to is what the Hopi value, hold high, set a value on; what they *think* is valuable. This may be because he has himself imbibed this fallacy and believes that all values are relative in the sense that there are no objective value facts but only value attitudes; or it may be that he merely follows here the sociological convention in the use of a sociological technical vocabulary. In any case, it represents a use of words which is likely to prejudice any issue of value theory before an attempt to think correctly about such issues is begun. We do not, of course, need to argue about any use of words, but it is necessary to insist on the difference between the *actual* value which a thing has and the *opinion* or *belief* someone has concerning that value—his *valuation* of that thing.

58

A good half of the current arguments offered in support of the cynical conclusion with respect to the normative rest on nothing more profound than this fallacy of ignoring or denying the difference between the value of a thing and the valuation of it. Sometimes this fallacy is committed at the start by *defining* 'good' or 'valuable' in terms of interests taken, or attitudes of favoring, or otherwise in terms merely of *valuations* made. We may be told, for example, that "X is good" *means* "I am in favor of X." Or we may be told that while the purpose of saying "X is red" is to convey information of an objective property—redness—which characterizes X, the purpose of saying "X is good" is to commend X to the hearer or induce him to favor X, and not to report any fact about the object at all. Sometimes these two are combined, and we are told that the purpose of ascribing value to X is to convey the speaker's attitude of favoring X *and* a hortation to the hearer to adopt the same attitude.

What any speaker may convey—evidence, give evidence of —by making his statement is one thing. What his purpose is in making the statement is another thing. And what the speaker says—asserts—is a third thing. And any semanticist who should confuse these three things, or substitute one of them for the other, seems unlikely to clarify any matter needing to be understood.

Let us take the examples "X is red" and "X is good." My saying "X is red" is good evidence for the truth of the different statement "I (the speaker) *believe* that X is red." But it is plainly false that my *statement* "X is red" *means* "I believe that X is red," because it could be true that X is red but false that I believe it, and it could be false that X is red but true that I believe it. Two statements which could under any circumstances be one of them false and the other true cannot mean the same thing. Whatever one means, it cannot, at one and the same time, be both true and false. Correspondingly, my saying "X is good" is quite reliable evidence for the truth of the different statement "I (the speaker) believe that X is good." But unless my believing it makes X good, or a thing's being good always and unfailingly makes me believe it good, these two statements simply cannot have the same meaning, since one of them could be true and the other false.

Similarly, my saying "X is good" is excellent evidence for the truth of the different statement "I (the speaker) am in favor of X." Clear-thinking and honest people do not favor a thing they believe to be bad, or call a thing good unless they are in favor of it. But if it is possible for clear-thinking people to make a *mistake* about the goodness of a thing, "X is good" *cannot mean* the same as "I (the speaker) am in favor of X." Common sense will add to this that these two statements do not mean the same thing anyway: we favor things *because* we believe them good, but they are not made good by our believing them good or by our favoring them.

It is likewise true that my saying "X is red" is quite reliable evidence that I want my hearer to believe that X is red, and that is a *part* at least of my purpose in saying it. Also, my saying "X is good" evidences my wish that the hearer should believe X good and be in favor of it. But occasionally a person of integrity might say, "This is good, but I do *not* want you to favor it or vote for it, because I know that *you* think it is bad, and I would not wish to persuade you to any attitude which is contrary to your own convictions." I do not want to assert here that the skeptic would say that such a statement as this last makes no sense whatever. But if it does make any kind of sense, then "X is good" and "I want you to favor X" simply cannot mean the same thing; and the former, "X is good," cannot even *imply* the latter, "I want you to favor X." If a statement, P, can be true when another, Q, is false, then it is also false that P implies Q.

Finally, we should notice that if my saying "X is good" evidences that I favor X, or that I wish my hearer to favor X, there are still three things to be noted about the relationship so evidenced: (1) it is not my statement made but my *act of stating it* which evidences my favoring or my wish that my hearer should favor it; (2) this act of mine does not logically imply anything (evidencing is not logical implying); and (3) one of two statements cannot mean the same thing as another unless each of them logically implies the other. The supposition that "X is good" means "I (the speaker) favor X" or "I want you to favor X," or the two of them together, simply will not bear logical or semantic examination. And, as I have attempted to show in the forepart of this lecture, the supposition that there is no objective goodness or badness of things which is a fact, independent of what anyone may think or say, is hardly more plausible than that "X is red" states no fact which is independent of what anyone may think or say about it.

All this leaves us with an attempted summary outline of the actual and valid foundation of judgments of moral rightness still before us. But I think that, with all these preliminaries now covered, the major considerations will prove simple enough to be outlined in the remaining lecture.

An Attempted Answer

If there are any valid moral dictates, then there must be certain ways of acting to which, when they affect others than the doer, it is genuinely imperative to conform, and other ways of acting which it is imperative to avoid. And it must further be the case that what ways of acting are thus morally right and what are morally wrong is some kind of fact which we are capable of knowing.

My approach to these questions has been roundabout. I have tried to show, first, that whatever it is right to do—in any sense of 'right to do'—is so because there is a justified expectation that the consequences of it will be good, and hence that what is right to do can be known if what is *good* is a determinable matter of fact which can be known.

But I have also spoken of those who are skeptical of this approach to questions of the moral because they doubt not only that anything is determinably right or wrong, in any deeper sense than that of being ways of acting of which we approve or disapprove, but doubt also that anything is either good or bad, in any deeper sense than that of being things which we favor and would recommend or things we disfavor and would recommend against.

I have not named any such skeptics of the normative at large—for two reasons. First, I do not have time here to present and do justice to the particular views and arguments of particular thinkers on the points at issue. (If in view of that omission you decide that I merely erect my own straw man to argue against, I shall not object to that.) But second, and more important—to me at least—I find it difficult to know, in the case of some who are thus skeptical, what they would say in answer to two questions I would put. First, is it or is it not rationally imperative to respect the aim of prudence? And if so, why the prudent but *not* the moral? Second, though I would not accuse anyone of denying that it is right and imperative to be logically consistent and cogent, and to avoid what contravenes the principles of logic, it is not clear to me how anyone who speaks of right and wrong in general can omit consideration of the logically right and wrong. And if there are valid imperatives of the logical sort, then why *not* of the moral?

For myself, I find that I must look to right and wrong in these other-than-moral senses in order to try to understand the ground of the moral validities. In this concluding lecture, I wish to suggest that all the different senses of 'right' and 'wrong' have a ground in common; that this ground lies, on the one side, in facts about the way the world is and, on the other, in the nature of man as an active being, capable of self-government, and one who determines whatever he does deliberately by reference to what he thinks, and what he expects as consequences of what he chooses to do. No such creature could, I think, rationally repudiate moral imperatives, just as he could not—unless perversely or irrationally—fail to respect the aim of prudence or the aim to be consistent and cogent in his thinking and concluding. And if, here, I continue to refer to a suppositious skeptic who doubts, it will be because I seem to find that the only conclusive proof of the validity of the basic principles of right is a kind of *reductio ad absurdum* of any attempt, on the part of self-governing creatures such as we humans are, to repudiate such principles. And, as I wish in conclusion to point out, the basic principles of morals are amongst such rationally nonrepudiable dictates.

Logic is the critique of ways of thinking and concluding, rather than of doing in the narrower sense of physical bringing about. But the deliberation of deliberate action is an essential part of it, and we take responsibility for this thinking part which determines the decision, as also we take responsibility for the physical and overt doing. In the thinking, there is the distinction between cogent and incogent—the distinction logic marks. Cogent thinking is logically justifiable thinking; incogent thinking is that which disregards or contravenes the rules of logic. Acts decided upon by incogent thinking will, by and large, be different acts than those determined by cogent thinking. Otherwise our thinking cogently would make no practical difference, no difference in what we choose to do. But that is unbelievable: if cogency makes no difference to our doing, and so has no consequence, of achievement or avoidance, in what happens in result, then why bother to be cogent? And also in that case, what would logic be, more than a game of analytic sentences which some play because they find it more amusing than acrostics? It is indeed a frequent defect in current logical theory that so often logic is spoken of as if it were no more than such a game, to be played according to certain accepted rules; and the significance of it as the critique of cogency, and of its rules as imperative to heed in coming to conclusions, is almost omitted from consideration. As a fact, being logical, cogent, has a use; it does some good. Being habitually incogent would be a sure road to practical disaster. Otherwise the question "Why be logical?" would have no answer.

Let us also observe that logic would have no use, and its principles would have no sanction, if there were no essential relation of what it dictates to objective fact. On this point, one use of it is exemplified by the fact that although one cannot actually fit a square peg to a round hole, one can try awfully hard. And the belief represented by a logically sanctioned conclusion is, similarly, one which, in the premises of it, could not possibly fail to be the fact.

To present any theory of normative judgments at large which should not cover the logically right must, I think, be extraordinary. But it would be equally extraordinary to say that "X is logically right" means "I (the speaker) disapprove of anyone's discrediting X." We do indeed disapprove of anyone's disbelieving the law of contradiction. But here, as elsewhere, this approval of what is right and disapproval of what is wrong is predicated upon something else which is as it is and not otherwise, regardless of what anybody should approve or disapprove. A logician might point out that a logical paradigm is certifiable merely from what it means, and to deny one is to make a self-contradictory statement, like "Something is both A and not-A." And he might add, if in a bad mood: "Your approval does not make the slightest difference to what is analytically certifiable. If you should disapprove it, so much the worse for you."

Let us further observe that inferring and concluding represents a department of our self-government. Deliberation is deliberate: that tautology has more than verbal significance. The summoning of premises relevant to an issue, and the testing of it by its relation to stored-up convictions gleaned from past experience, does not do itself. And as we have observed already, the deliberation of deliberate action is continuous with the doing of it, and our responsibility for this deliberation of it is a part of our responsibility for the act.

By reason of these obvious considerations, one who should deny that there are any valid imperatives of right doing would be subject to a certain *argumentum ad hominem*—one which there is no fallacy in urging against him, because he must take responsibility for his own conclusions and for his own arguing to them. The skeptical thesis itself is advanced as a deliberate conclusion, and it must be one which is justified and right or unjustified and unwarranted. And once the argument advanced in support of it is before us, this skeptical conclusion is either one it is rationally imperative for us to accept, or one which, by reason of incogency, fails of its purpose. The skeptic's advancement of his own argument is a deliberate and governed activity on his part. It is a physical activity even, a piece of deliberate and overt doing. There are supposed to be rules about it, rules of valid inference. But the skeptical conclusion argued for is that there are *no* valid rules and *no* valid imperatives of the right government of action. And now we must ask the skeptic just why he expects us to feel constrained to accept this conclusion which his argument seeks to establish. He has, in the conclusion itself, repudiated all valid imperatives constraining anybody to do anything, and encouraged us to think that he himself rejects constraint by any rules of right upon his conduct. Why, then, should he expect us to be abashed of our previous conviction and, in the light of his argument, give it up? Why should we not rather say to one another, "I don't like this fellow's slant on things: let's ask him to stop interrupting our serious attempt to think straight on this matter." As a fact, one who should repudiate the imperative to respect cogency in argument would forfeit his license to participate in any forum where thinking is regarded as a serious business.

If there be those who speak of right and wrong in general, but when we come to believing and concluding and arguing would say, "Oh, but we did not mean to include cogency and the logically right; that's different," I shall have to reply that I do not find it different, but very much the same, and an excellent example of the fact that there are valid imperatives of the right the repudiation of which would be silly. If they should urge that the logical is not a matter of what I call validity but of analytic truth, then I must reply that my point concerns exactly the question whether there are or are not imperatives we are bound to respect. And if the truth is just a little different matter, *respect* for the truth is still precisely to the point: there is the silly question "Why respect the truth? Is it always imperative to respect the truth?" If they say "Yes" to that, they admit one binding imperative of rational human conduct. If they say "No," they render themselves and anything they may assert suspect. To argue for the conclusion "There are no binding imperatives of conduct" commits a practical contradiction.

I must ask you to observe the precise nature of this manner of self-contradiction, because it is frequently misunderstood. It is *not* a logical contradiction implied by the *proposition* asserted; instead it is an incompatibility of the predictable consequences of *asserting* this proposition with the presumptive purpose of this act of assertion. The ancient and much discussed example is that of Epimenides, who, being himself a Cretan, asserted that all Cretans are liars. Observe that the proposition he uttered has no logical implication which is contradictory of it; if someone else in the gathering had said, "Epimenides is a Cretan, and all Cretans are liars," it would have been a bit implausible but certainly not a logical contradiction. But when an admitted Cretan says "All Cretans are liars," he brands his own statement as deserving no credence on the ground of his making it. (Please observe here that I am *not* discussing such a statement as "Everything I say is false": that statement *is* a logical self-contradiction; but the historic paradox of Epimenides is not.) The paradox lies in the fact that a presumptive purpose of making any statement is that the hearers should believe it. But anyone hearing Epimenides make his statement, and initially inclined to believe what he says, would instead be moved to discredit this and any other statement that he makes. If intended to induce belief, the act of asserting or implying "I am a liar" is an essentially self-frustrating act; what is so said defeats the purpose of saying it. Any assertion or other act which has this character I will call a pragmatic contradiction.

Now let us observe that anyone who should assert or imply that there is no valid imperative to be logical, consistent, cogent, similarly gives notice that nothing *he* says is to be regarded as governed by any intention to adhere to the cogent and believable, and to avoid what is fallacious and warrants no credence. And he also gives notice that either he misreads his own nature or there is no reason to consider his conclusions seriously on the ground of his advancing them or arguing for them. And one who asserts "There are no normative judgments which are genuinely valid" falls into exactly that predicament, because any judgment of a statement made or conclusion drawn as being cogent and believable must necessarily be such a normative judgment. Such attempted repudiation of the normative at large can only be an adventure in intellectual self-frustration, denying in words what we cannot avoid assuming in practice, if we draw any distinction between

68

the fallacious and the cogent. We cannot repudiate governing principles of our self-determined activity because we cannot abdicate our autonomy of decision; and self-government implies self-constraint. Without acknowledgment of the normative and imperative to respect, we make ourselves out to be irrational—either foolish or perverse.

However, although these considerations make evident that it is not possible to deny, rationally, that there are normative judgments which are valid, still they are not sufficient, by themselves, to establish the validity of any further and particular imperatives such as those of prudence or of morals. Since thinking and believing must be involved in any decision of doing, the logical validities are a *necessary* condition of any validity of principles of prudence or of morals, but they do not constitute a *sufficient* condition of the validity of prudential or moral dictates.

That the further discussion called for cannot be fully set forth here will go without saying. But I think that the salient points can be suggested. It is only the imperatives of prudence, and of the moral as the imperative to respect the interests of others, which will need to be considered further. As we have already seen, all the diverse rules of technically right doing represent ways of achieving particular ends which are taken for granted as sometimes justified to pursue. Such rules of technically right doing are imperative to heed if and when the technical ends are right ones to pursue. But this further question of their being, on any occasion, rightly chosen ends, is, eventually, a question of somebody's prudentially justified aim, or of the moral justification of somebody's intended doing. Any further question will, thus, concern the prudential or the moral justification of deliberate acts.

First, let us ask whether what it is prudent to do is a matter of knowledge, a matter of determinable fact. We have already reviewed, in our second lecture, the premises for answering that question. The prudential end is, by definition, the doer's own good. And one thing must be obvious beyond all doubt. Nobody could possibly do himself any good unless he should know what he would find good in case he should achieve it. Nor could he do himself any good without knowing what acts open to him would bring about such good consequences. To be sure, any doer, when called upon to take a prudent decision, could make a mistake, on either of these two points. But that possibility of mistake goes along with the nature of knowledge itself, which being directed upon something which is as it is and not otherwise, regardless of our thinking, is by the same token always liable to mistake. Also we have already covered the point that such predictive knowledge cannot be, theoretically, better than probable, but that the justified assessment of it as probable justifies acting on it. No skeptic who does not challenge the validity of empirical knowledge in general can well deny the cognitive character of prediction of the consequences of our acts. The boggle here, for current skepticism, is that it wishes to affirm the cognitive character of predictions generally, but to exclude predictions of the good or bad, because it wishes to deny the cognitive character of all apprehensions of the evaluative kind, in contrast to, *e.g.*, apprehensions of the red or round. But that point also we have covered. I will add here only that whatever is presently envisaged and could be recognized if later found is cognitively subject to prediction. On this point, the skeptic seems to be reduced to asserting that we don't know what we expect in expecting something to be good or cannot recognize the expected goodness when we achieve it. About that, nobody—skeptical or not—knows more than you do. I leave it to you.

I must deal with the parallel question whether our judgments of the right to do are cognitive, with equal abruptness. Here again, much of the argument has been anticipated. We have not yet considered what, precisely, moral dictates dictate. But certainly they involve consideration of the good or bad consequences to others of what we do. And the supposition that we cannot know, with probability at least, what acts of ours will result in good or bad to others has the implausible implication that we cannot, by the utmost endeavor, deliberately benefit anybody else or do him any harm. Here again, the skeptic will, if judicious, wish to admit that there is possible knowledge of the causal connection between the act and its consequences, but will balk at calling it knowledge of any manner of *right* or *wrong* doing, because he is committed to deny the cognitive character of apprehension of the results as being good or bad, and hence to deny the cognitive character of judgment of the act which predictably will lead to good or bad results as right or wrong. And here again, I leave the matter to your own further reflection—except for one crucial point.

The point reserved is the consideration that recognition of anything as wrong carries with it an imperative to refrain from doing it, and recognition of anything as right may imply an imperative to do. The previous point was that *what* it will be prudent to do, and *what* it will be morally justified to do, cannot help but be a matter for cognitive determination. But it is a subtly different question—"*Why* is it imperative to be prudent?", and it is also a different question—"*Why* is it imperative to be moral?"

The definitive nature of prudence—our concept of prudence—is exhibited and delineated by the maxim of prudence: So act as to maximize your possible realizations of the good, as against the bad, in your life as a whole. And as this implies: Do no act which will sacrifice a future and greater good to any lesser and more immediate good. Concerning the question *"Why* is it imperative to be prudent, or as prudent as is compatible with being moral?", or the question *"Is* it imperative to respect the aim of prudence?", I am tempted to say, "Well, you tell me: you know as much about it as anybody does." I am also tempted to repeat something which John Stuart Mill said—most incautiously. In substance what he said was: "The only proof that anything is visible is that somebody sees it. I conceive that, in like manner, the only proof it is possible to give that something is desirable, is that people do desire it." But that incautious statement of Mill's is a prime target of the sophomore. Somebody has recently called it "Mill's Notorious Analogy." What I think expresses Mill's intended point, and will say myself, is: nothing could be proved to be *intrinsically* desirable unless those who should possess it would *find* it desirable to possess. That I have already implied in my discussion of the intrinsically good. If relation to what will, if achieved, conduce to the experience of goodness, does not justify action, then no act nor anything else is either justified or unjustified.

But there is something just a little further to be said on this point about prudence. I shall try to say it briefly.

One who should repudiate respect for the prudential aim must find himself in the same kind of predicament as one who says "I have no respect for logical cogency"—what I have called a pragmatic contradiction. The Cyrenaics (remember) did, in words, repudiate all prudence, saying, "Catch pleasure as it flies; have no thought for the morrow." Now please notice that the Cyrenaic is recommending a comprehensive and continuing attitude toward life; and presumably he is adopting it himself. This recommendation is: In the future, let us repudiate all constraint upon our action by reason of any concern for the future. But this is a *resolution*, concerning and presumably constraining our future action. No resolution makes any kind of sense unless it is intended to constrain our future action to accord with it. But the advice of *this* resolution is that hereafter we repudiate *all* constraint upon our following the inclination to pleasure at the moment in question. And that calls for repudiation in the future of any constraint exercised by any resolution we may previously have made. Please note the Cyrenaic's predicament here. He resolves that in the future he will heed no resolution which could constrain his momentary inclination to immediate pleasure. But this directs that in the future he should never be constrained by any antecedent resolution he may have previously taken. So if he heeds *this* resolution, he must at once repudiate it if, at any later date, his having taken it should threaten to have any influence upon his conduct. The simpler way of putting the point is that one who is capable of deliberate action cannot, in the nature of the case, repudiate concern for the future. The past is gone and cannot be altered. And the present is already what it is and not otherwise. There is nothing but the future which any deliberate action could affect. And one who should repudiate concern for the future would do no deliberate act at all. That is one attitude which no human could possibly take. There is one principle no self-governing creature can adopt—the principle of having no principles. There is one imperative he cannot heed—the imperative to heed no imperatives; one resolution he cannot follow—the resolution to disregard all resolutions. If the skeptic is *not* recommending his own negative attitude as the one which is right and which all of us ought to take, and his own negative conviction

as correct and imperative for us to believe, then why should
he take himself seriously—or ask us to? And if he *is* urging
it as imperative to disbelieve in valid imperatives, then—!
Or do we overlook the possibility that he may be, like Epimenides, speaking only for his own and our amusement?

Let us turn to the moral. The question "Why be prudent?"
may seem slightly silly on the face of it, since in point of fact
no one fails to desire the prudential end of a good life for himself. But the question "Why be moral?" does not have quite
this same air of the prima facie gratuitous. One can more
seriously ask why one should trench upon the aim of a good
life for himself in order not to encroach upon the similar aim
of others. I shall suggest, however, that so to phrase it is the
wrong way to put this basic question of the validity of the
moral imperative. If we would find an answer, the better way
to put it is to ask why we should restrict ourselves to ways of
acting which we should willingly see others adopt as well.

There is one fact of life which, theoretically, could be
omitted in the consideration of the ground of the prudential
imperative, but can *not* be omitted in considering the ground
of the moral: the fact, namely, that human life is social. A
Robinson Crusoe with no man Friday, or even any dog or
parrot, would still have his problems of prudence, but he
need have no problems of the distinctively moral. Moral problems are predicated on the presumption that a human life is
to be lived in a society of one's fellows, in which the acts of
each affect the lives of others. And the sense and meaning of
'fellow' here is that of another who is like oneself in standing
under the necessity to determine his own acts deliberately
and self-critically, having and respecting his own prudential
end, and obliged to consider, and in some measure formulate, his own maxims for his own self-government.

As in the case of prudence there is one comprehensive maxim which sums up the prudential aim, so also with the moral there is one comprehensive formula which is definitive of the essence of the moral. That comprehensive principle is, in the most lucid and readily applicable statement of it, "Do unto others as you would that others should do unto you." That rule, by itself, dictates no specific way of acting, fronting any particular problem of what to do. It says only: "Remember your social situation, and remember that nothing can be a way of acting it is justified for you to adopt unless it is equally a justified way of acting for any other person to adopt, fronting this problem which you face and in the same premises of action. A valid rule is a valid rule, no matter who you are."

There could be no apter statement of this definitive dictate of the moral; but perhaps those who have to contend with moral skeptics may be excused for wanting to spell it out a little. Kant, in his famous formulation of the Categorical Imperative, phrases it: "So act that you could will the maxim of your conduct to become a universal law." He also puts it in another form—believing, of course, that this comes to the same thing: "So act as always to treat humanity, whether in your own person or that of any other, always as an end withal, and never as a means only." I offer still another formulation, to which I would assign the same intent: "Do no act which contravenes any rule which you would call upon other men to respect and conform to."

Omitting the verbal considerations, let us explore the common intent of these different formulations of the basic moral law. First, it is implied that it is the good or harm of an act to those affected by it which should weigh. The Golden Rule covers that point by challenging us to think of ourselves as *suffering* this act at the hands of another; and if our so suffering it would lead us to call upon the doer of it to refrain, then to refrain from doing it ourselves. And our so thinking of the act as done to ourselves by another reminds us that the rightness or wrongness pertains to the character of the act itself, impersonally considered. Circumstances which are personal may have their weight. For example, things it is right for an officer of the law to do, or for a skilled physician, might be wrong for others. And things it might be right to do to a criminal may be wrong to do to an innocent person. The problem of statement is to eliminate what is personal *in the manner of the weighing* without eliminating what may be personal in *what is to be weighed*.

Let us suppose, for simplicity, that the act in question will affect only three persons: John, Mary, and oneself. To state fully the problem to be weighed, set down under the headings "John," "Mary," and "Myself" everything pertinent to each which is a relevant consideration for the doing or not doing of this kind of act. Then substitute the letters A, B, and C for the personal designations. Your test, then, for determining whether this act is right for you to do is the question whether you would equally approve it whether your position in the matter should be that of A, B, or C. It is in *that* sense that whatever is morally right to do is right regardless of who does it or to whomsoever it is done. The moral law is no respecter of particular persons, but a respecter of all alike. Even in following that test, it would still be possible to misjudge this impersonal character of the act as morally right or wrong—for any number of reasons, including possible wrong prediction of its consequences, or a possible lack of imagination in appreciation of their quality as gratifying or grievous to those affected. On such points, we may back up the moral law, or spell it out, by supplementary and subordinate rules, beaten out in the course of experience, and accepted as representing what will be in accord with this basic principle in particular kinds of cases. (The frequently quoted moral dictates, such as "Tell no lies" and "Keep your promises," are such subordinate rules of thumb for moral guidance.) But there is no other and final test of what is morally right than this basic principle; and no test having different import could be final.

One amazing thing about this rule, if we stop to think of it, is that, though in one sense it demands so much and is a counsel of perfection—whatever you think it would be universally right to do, do that—in another sense it demands so little. It is even a subordinate question, under the jurisdiction of it, at what point, or on points of what kind, interests which are personal and prudential must give way to the social interest of all affected. Even a philosophical egoist, if he be a man of integrity like Bentham, and thinks that there is no rule of conduct higher than prudence, does not approve the repudiation of *all* binding rules of action; instead he announces unqualified pursuit of the prudential and first-personal interest as that rule whose acceptance and conformity to, on the part of everybody, he would approve. We may well think that Bentham's error lay in ascribing spontaneously benevolent feelings like his own to men in general, and poorly envisaging what life would be like in a society in which the rule of unrestrained egoism should universally prevail. On that point, one may think that Hobbes had the better imagination: life among those who did not contract away some part of their original egoistic privilege, and were not already bound to the rule of keeping their promises made, would be nasty, brutish, and short.

Even the emotivist could crawl under the Kantian tent, and recognize the Categorical Imperative as implicit in his interpretation of right and wrong. If "X is right" means "I approve of X as a way of doing and an active attitude: do you so as well," the same cautionary observation is implicit as that which attends any application of the Golden Rule: "Approve only of such doing as you would willingly see others approve as well." The emotivist must be careful of what he approves and recommends to the approval of others, lest their taking his advice might make him sorry by the results. The emotive contagion which he seeks to promote must rationally be submitted to critique by reference to the question "How would you come off, and how would you like it, if everybody *should* behave as you suggest?" It is even a reasonable extrapolation, which he could hardly refuse, to go the whole length and say, "Approve only of that which you could will that all men approve of and adopt." And that is just what the Categorical Imperative says. But the Categorical Imperative emphasizes this point which the emotivist seems to forget—namely, the rational constraint upon doing what emotive feelings prompt which is implicit in the criticizing thought: "But what if everybody *should* do so as well; how would you like that?" In other words, it may be affective feeling which inclines or prompts us to the act; but it is what we call our rationality which provides the test of justified choosing to do and gives the rule. The emotivist appears to forget which is boss, the affective feeling which prompts, or the rational and cognitive deliberation which criticizes. Men, like other animals, are inclined to do simply what they feel like doing. But in distinction from other animals, they have the capacity sometimes to do otherwise than to follow such impulses and immediate promptings—the capacity to direct their own action by foresight of results, and adjudicate them by reference to what they call good (valid) reasons. That is what it means to be an active and self-governing creature. And as we observed at the outset, men being endowed with this rational and critical capacity *must* on occasion decide their own action: as often as they realize that alternatives are open to them, they must choose what they shall do. And we cannot but recognize that our choosing one as against another alternative calls for some justification of the choosing. Also, recognizing our likeness to other men, on these fundamental points, we cannot fail to acknowledge that whatever will justify us in choosing what we do must be such as would, in identically the same premises of action, justify any other man in taking that same decision, acting in that same way. Justified doing must, in identically the same premises, be the same for all men, in the same sense that justified believing must, in identically the same premises, be the same for all men. In both cases, the only finally good excuse for disagreement of conviction is some difference in the premises which are open to us, or are relevant to our individual decision. Both in decisions of belief and in decisions to do we recognize, in recognizing rationality as common to us all, that the premises being the same, the convictions should be the same, or at least compatible with one another. If that fails to be the case, then somebody must be *wrong*.

Failure to recognize this primacy of the rational critique over the immediate and affective promptings of action is one basic fault which I would charge against the emotivist type of ethical theory. But I should wish it to be observed that in that kind of *reductio ad absurdum* which I think holds against any theory which is skeptical of the validity of normative judgments, I appeal to certain premises as implicit. This type of argument is, as I have acknowledged, also an *argumentum ad hominem—ad hominem* in the sense in which '*Hominem*' may be spelled with a capital and means to denote the genus *homo*. It appeals to facts about the common nature of man which are open to all of us in a reflective examination of the kind of creatures that we are, and which I think that any such examination which is judicious must compel us to recognize as the truth about ourselves. The *reductio ad absurdum* which proceeds by exposing an implicit pragmatic contradiction must, in the end, appeal to such self-consciousness of active and self-governing creatures.

I find one other small point—or perhaps it is not so small—on which the implications of an emotivist theory wound me in my conceit of myself as a human being. Recognizing that, on their theory, there can be no justified convictions on points of moral and otherwise normative judgments, the emotivists still leave open the privilege of hortation, recommendation, and something they may refer to as persuasion as substitute for the attempt to *convince* others, in case of disagreement. I suppose it to be a common attitude amongst us, and one which is justified, that we do not intend to allow ourselves to be induced to agree by any appeal which is acknowledged to be addressed to our emotive feelings simply, instead of to our recognition of cogency in thinking and concluding. And there again, I point out that I have capitalized upon the supposition that you share my repugnance to an appeal to emotive "persuasion" as against an appeal to reason. I have appealed to it in my *argumentum ad hominem*, which presumes that he who argues without the supposition that his conclusion will be imperative for us to accept on grounds of its *cogency* forfeits all claim to our agreement. My argument touching that point will not have satisfied you unless—as I admit suspecting—you agree with me already about sufficient reasons for changing one's mind.

But if, in view of the acknowledgments I have just made, you should be minded to say that my whole argument now stands revealed as not only an *argumentum ad Hominem* (spelled with a capital "H") but also a *petitio principii,* I shall not attempt to fend off that accusation, but instead will ask, "What other kind of proof would you ask for, touching the very foundations of the right and valid?" No conclusion about the right, or about anything else—X—can be drawn from premises which do not themselves, explicitly or implicitly, say anything about the right, or about X. And while less general statements about X can often be inferred from the more general, this order of deduction cannot be reversed. In consequence, what is most general, most comprehensive in its scope, most nearly ultimate, concerning any topic, cannot be proved at all, unless by some manner of observation or some *reductio ad absurdum* of denying it. And though it may not have been generally remarked, it is nevertheless the fact that even such proof by the method of *reductio ad absurdum,* when addressed to ultimates, must be, in a queer kind of way, a begging of the question.

Logic makes a good example. No conclusion of logic can be derived from premises which say nothing about the logical. And how should one *prove* any first premises for *logic?* They can be proved by showing that the contradictory of any logical principle is itself a self-contradictory statement, and one which also implies the principle which it contradicts. But of course you will have to appeal to principles of logic in drawing this and other inferences. Any proof of logic will beg the question of the basic logical validities. Or to put what is really the same point in another way: How should you embarrass anyone who denied the validity of logic merely by showing that what he asserts is not logically cogent? How could you convict anybody of being wrong in denying the validity of the distinction between right and wrong? Such a sinner against the light of reflective self-consciousness is embarrassmentproof. Nothing short of violence would hurt his feelings. But is it anything against the necessary truth of logic that you can't prove it without begging the question? And is it anything against the validity of the distinction between right and wrong that the first principles of the right— in any particular sense of 'right'—cannot be proved without somehow begging the question? It is in recognition of such considerations that I have said that there is no final proof of the validity of any species of norms except by appeal to what is involved in being human, and an active, self-governing being. In the case of the moral, I can only say finally that one who does not acknowledge it as imperative to behave in that same way in which he would call upon other men generally to behave is irrational, as one who denies the law of contradiction is irrational, and one who should find prudence a matter of no concern is irrational. And one who is *not* thus perverse must acknowledge the validity of the Golden Rule as something more compelling than emotive feeling or a sentimental persuasion.

SELECTED PAPERS

Values and Facts

It is values and their relation to facts which constitute our topics here, and presumably what a fact is is to be taken for granted. But in view of common ambiguities, brief observation of what the word 'fact' designates may be in order.

I take it that a fact is what makes some true proposition true: for every true proposition there is some corresponding fact, and every fact is expressible by some proposition which is true. A fact is something which is the case. Its being the case is independent of anybody's mention of it and independent of anybody's apprehension or misapprehension of it, but by its nature it must be propositionally formulatable. In that, a fact is distinguished from an object or an event. Objects exist, and the existence or nonexistence of any mentioned object is a fact. But the object itself is not a fact, and to say that a fact exists or does not exist is bad grammar. Similarly, events are not facts. An event happens or takes place, or a mentioned event may be one which never happens. The happening or nonhappening of an event is a fact. But the fact does not happen or fail to happen. If it is said that an object or event is a fact, what is meant is that the object exists or the event occurs.

Anything cognized is a fact, if the cognition is veridical and the formulation of what is so apprehended would be a true statement. If we allow the common assumption, then to say that anything is known implies that what is so cognized is a fact, since common sense calls for the veracity of any cognition which is to be called knowledge. But it follows from this, as from any other reasonable manner of conceiving knowledge, that to speak of an object or event as being known is, strictly, bad grammar, even if that idiom is commonly allowed. We must regard that as a customary figure of speech or abbreviation, intending to assert the existence of a cognized object or the occurrence of a cognized event or—more frequently—that some fact is known concerning an existent object or an event which occurs. Any object which exists and any event which happens will have certain characters or properties and not have other characters or properties. That an object which exists or an event which happens has or lacks a certain property or character is a fact. But the property, like the object or event, is not a fact. If we say that a property is factual, we mean that it is instanced—that something has it, or that a particular thing has it.

Amongst the characters of objects and events are the times and places of their existence or occurrence. Both objects and events have space-time boundaries. But facts have no date or locus: once a fact, always a fact; and what is anywhere a fact is everywhere a fact. More precisely, the ascription of time or place to a fact is bad grammar, though times and places may be constituents in facts.

There is one requirement which must be met in speaking of objects, events, properties, and facts: it must be possible to think incorrectly and to make false statements which still are not nonsense. It must be possible to speak, with grammatical correctness, of objects that do not exist, events that do not happen, properties which are not instanced, and to ascribe prop-

erties to things which do not have them. This whole matter
can be covered if we recognize, for objects designated, for oc-
currences referred to, for properties mentioned, and for what
is expressed as being the case, the one grand dichotomy of
actual or nonactual. We shall not, however, thus get rid of
linguistic paradoxes: there *are* no nonactual entities, and in
common parlance "is an X" means "is an actual X," and "is a
fact" means "is an actual fact." But no sinuosity of theory can
obviate the circumstance that nonactual entities are thought
of and may be mentioned, and that nonactual facts not only
are mentioned but can be asserted—in false statements. Recognition that what is nonactual can, for any category, be mentally entertained as if it were actual is unavoidable. If, then,
one *mentions* as fact what is not fact, he does not necessarily
commit an error; his whole statement which includes such
mention may be true. But one who *states* as fact what is not
(actual) fact makes a false statement. And that nonactual
facts can be spoken of and asserted leaves it still the case that
every (actual) fact is as it is and not otherwise, regardless of
anybody's knowledge or misapprehension of it.*

The word 'value', like the word 'color' or 'shape', is used to
designate a category of properties which things exhibit. And
the plural 'values' is properly used to refer to species or varieties of this generic property value, as 'colors' is used to refer

---

* That this matter, so hastily covered, is more complex than our discussion here indicates will be obvious. In particular, there is the question
whether 'fact' should be extended to what is asserted by analytic statements
or restricted to what empirical statements assert. I would not impose this
restriction: there are facts of the relation of meanings, and analytic statements express them.

I have elsewhere used 'state of affairs' in the sense here assigned to 'fact'.
But that has led to misunderstanding on the part of some, who think of
states of affairs as having space-time boundaries. Even empirical facts have
no such bounds.

to species or varieties or the generic property color. The species of color have one-word names: 'red', 'orange', 'yellow', —; but the names of species of value are compound: 'aesthetic value', 'economic value', and so on. Any species of value may properly be spoken of as "a value," as any species of color is spoken of as "a color." And just as any species of color is subject to further specification, and there are varieties of red, such as crimson lake, the species of value are subject to further specification, e.g., aesthetic value may be musical value or literary value. Also, just as a variety of any species of color is properly called a color, so a variety of any species of value is properly called a value. Any discriminable color-character is a color, and any discriminable value-character is a value.

Unlike color, but like truth or probability, the things of which a value-character is truly predicable are themselves sometimes spoken of as 'values'; but let us decide that in the case of value this is improper usage, and if one speaks of that which has a value as itself a value he is to be excused as understandable but imprecise.

Unlike color and shape, but like brightness and probability, whatever has a value has a degree of value: whatever is valuable is more or less valuable than some other things, as whatever is bright is more or less bright than some other things. And like probability, but unlike brightness, a degree of disvalue may be spoken of as a degree of value. Also as in the case of probability, usage so varies on this last point as to constitute an ambiguity of language. But let us here allow ourselves to speak of value in this sense of value-or-disvalue if on occasion that makes for brevity and will not be misleading.

A more important concern is the category or categories of entities of which value is predicable. I take it that ascriptions of value would be altogether meaningless if it were not for the fact that humans, like other animals, enjoy and suffer and find their experience affected with the qualities of gratification or grief, satisfaction or aversion. But humans, as well as other creatures, learn to identify objects and properties of objects, and happenings in the external world and properties of such objective events, as causative agencies productive of these qualities of their experience. And 'good' and 'bad', and other value-terms, are extended to those objective things and properties of them which are identified as causing the character of direct experience which is found immediately satisfying and good, or immediately dissatisfying and bad. Thus the generic value-terms, as well as some which are more specific, have two distinguishable senses: (1) as applying to passages of experience and signifying their immediately gratifying or grievous quality, and (2) as applying to objective entities—objects, events, or properties of objects or events—and signifying *potentialities* of these entities for leading to experiences having the quality of the gratifying and pleasing or of the grievous and displeasing. To say that an experience is pleasing means one thing, and to say that the object which pleases is pleasing means something different. For one point, the experience is transitory, but the object is more or less enduring and may affect experience again. For another, every experience is personal and private, but an object may affect the experience of many persons. To say that the experience which pleases is a pleasing experience is a tautology. But to say that an object which pleases is a pleasing object is not a tautology: it may displease us on another occasion, and may displease other persons. To say that an object is pleasing means that it is characteristically capable of producing pleasure in the experience of those who experience it. Or if this is a dubious explication of 'pleasing' as a predicate of objects—since we say occasionally that an object is pleasing meaning only that it pleases under present circumstances—at least 'valuable' and generic ascriptions of value to objective entities are less subject to such ambiguity.

The value of an experience or experience-content is simply the value-quality which is found in it. An experience is a *passage* of experience, a conscious event or event of consciousness. The experience is transitory, but the occurrence of it with the quality found is a fact—a datum-fact and, for him whose experience it is and at the time of its occurrence, an indubitable fact. This fact is not transitory; no fact is transitory. What is thus immediately apprehended, and is fact, one may later forget or misremember, and at anytime it may be unknown to or misjudged by others. Presumably, any immediate fact of one's experience later becomes less than certain and less credible because remembered; and the facts of one's experience are, for others, no better than probable, being determined by inferences from observed behavior. But the fact of any immediate experience characterized by value or disvalue remains as it is and not otherwise, regardless of anybody's possible ignorance or misjudgment.

There are those who deny all datum-facts immediately disclosed and—consistently with their own account—are never sure whether they are gratified or grieved, as also they are never certain whether they see red or feel cold, or whether they are just now alive. But any such objector will at least admit that disclosures of experience are as near to certain as any empirical fact that we can apprehend. Amongst them are the values ascribable to direct and present experience. What is thus valuable, be it noted, is the *occurrence* of this experience characterized by the positive value-quality, the fact of it.

Further, it is of first importance that we should be able to predict, with a measure of assurance, the value-qualities to be realized in future and possible experience. Such predictions, like predictions generally, are no better than probable when made. But it is only as we are able to make trustworthy predictions of this type that we can so govern action as to serve our future happiness and avoid unhappiness. Without some measure of control over the value-quality of our future living, any capacity to affect the future in other respects would be worthless. What we so predict as a value-quality of future experience either is an actual fact or it is not. And, unlike predictions of objective facts, the predictions of our own experience will be decisively verified or decisively falsified by the experience predicted, when it comes. Also, it is only as we can, with some assurance, predict the value-effect of our actions upon the experience of others that we can do them any good or any harm. And what we so predict is likewise fact or not fact, though predictions of the experience of others are not decisively verifiable for us, but only as highly confirmable as their behavior may allow us later to infer.

The consideration that predictions of the value-quality of our own experience are, when put to the test, decisively verified or falsified is of first importance, not only for its bearing upon rational decisions of action, but also because such findings of value in experience constitute our most nearly decisive confirmations of the values ascribed to objective entities. That an object has the potentiality for producing satisfaction or dissatisfaction in experience is best proved by finding that quality in experiences affected by it.

We should observe, however, that ascription to experience of a value or disvalue which resides in its immediate quality as gratifying or as grievous does not represent the only sense in which values are attributable to experiences. Passages of experience not only have such immediately found goodness and badness in themselves, but they also make their contribution of good or bad to that life on the whole in which they are ingredient. A good life could not be constituted exclusively of dissatisfying experiences; nor could any life made up exclusively of gratifying passages of experience be a bad one to live. But for a variety of reasons which, being familiar, need not be recited here, an immediately dissatisfying experience may be salutary and contribute more to the goodness of a life than any alternative to it, while an immediate gratification on a particular occasion may be notably prejudicial to the goodness of that life in which it is constituent.

The goodness of life, or of *a* life, on the whole, is the *final* good, the *summum bonum*. So far as we can control or affect our experience, we accept it as rational to subordinate our interest in the quality of any experience as immediate to our interest in as good a life as we can achieve; and we seek to determine action so as to bring about or allow the realization of a possible experience by reference to the contribution it will make to a good life rather than by reference merely to its immediate quality as gratifying or as grievous. Let us call this value or disvalue which an experience may have as contributing to the final end of a good life the *contributory* value of that experience. And let us note in passing that, unlike value as immediately found, contributory value must be judged and may be misjudged; and unlike value as ascribed to predicted experiences and decisively verifiable by later findings, the contributory value of any experience is confirmable only as various of its consequences for our further living are realized. Any judgment of what will make for a good life is, indeed, notably complex and hazardous. But however difficult to assess, the contributory value of any experience is a fact about it, which is as it is and not otherwise, regardless of anybody's judgment or misjudgment of it. It is a kind of fact which we continually—and rationally must—seek to determine, in the interest of a good life for ourselves, or for anyone else whose happiness concerns us.

The judgment of contributory value resembles the judgment of values as attributable to objects, events, and properties of objects and events, in being an empirical judgment based on evidence drawn from past experience and, like empirical judgments generally, no better than probable. But the modes in which value is attributed to objective entities are more various and more complex than those in which value is ascribed to experiences and the content of them. We assess the value of objective things in different ways for different purposes. *Personal* values—value to me, value to you, value to subject S— are assessed by reason of the personal differences and differences of personal circumstances affecting the values which a particular objective entity may have for an individual and as affecting individual experience. *Impersonal* or *social* values are assessed as values to men at large or to the community. As a cross-classification to those just mentioned, values in objective things are divisible into inherent values and instrumental values. An *inherent* value of an object is a property of the object conducive to the realization of positive value-quality in the presence of that object itself. Aesthetic values exemplify inherent value. *Instrumental* value is the value of a thing as conducive to positive value-quality realizable not in the experience of that thing itself but of some other thing or things whose production or availability for experience it facilitates. The various utilities and kinds of utility which objects have illustrate the instrumental value of objective entities. There are other and more specific modes in which values are ascribed to objects and events, and observation of them would have its importance for the understanding of linguistic usages in value-predication, but consideration of these must be omitted.

What is true of all such modes of the attribution of value to objective entities is that positive value is ascribed according as the entity in question is judged capable of contributing, or likely to contribute, to the positive value-quality of experiences directly or indirectly affected by it. An object which, so far as the existence of it should affect any life, would always operate to enhance, and never to detract from, the gratifying quality of experience would be a superlatively good thing of its kind; and any object has value according as its potentialities for affecting experience are of that sort. The same is true for objective entities in general. This is the generic sense of 'value' as ascribed to external actualities.

If it be thought anomalous that value as predicable of objective things should be identified with a potentiality of them for producing experiences of a specific sort, let us observe that a similar account may be given for any other property or character verifiably attributable to an object. No object can be determined to have a certain color or shape, or any other ascribable property, in any other manner than, eventually, by the finding of some quality or qualities in experience affected by that object. The objective character of things can be learned or verified in no other way. Only by understanding what empirical findings will be evidence that object O has the character C, and what findings will be evidence that O does not have C, can we verify or confirm any such truth about external things at all. But an object which is red or round does not continuously manifest this objective character by producing visual experiences of red or round; it produces such specific evidence only under certain subjective and objective conditions of observation. And this obvious consideration emphasizes the fact that this property which the object continuously and verifiably has is correctly describable as a potentiality for producing experiences of a specific quality or character, or experiences having different characters under different conditions. These are our only possible evidence of the property ascribed. On that point, there is no basic difference between value as a property of objects and other objective properties they can be known to have.

By the same token, value-determinations, given the meanings here assigned to them, represent a species of empirical knowledge. The occurrence of value-quality in immediate experience is an empirical datum-fact when that experience is given, and does not need to be judged. The ascription of such value-quality to any future experience is an empirical prediction, verifiable or falsifiable in the experience predicted. The contributory value of an experience and all values ascribable to objects are empirical facts to be judged on grounds of experience and confirmed by predictable experiences, as empirical and objective facts in general are to be judged and confirmed. And if it should be said by some that 'value' as here explicated does not coincide with the real meaning of 'value', then at least it represents a possible meaning, whether real or conventional, and one which is true to certain identifiable and important facts of life. It also has whatever advantage goes with identifying valuations as a type of empirical findings and judgments whose truth or falsity is as demonstrable as other types of empirical findings and judgments, and in the same general fashion.

The skeptical doubts about value as an objective category should, I think, be obviated by these considerations. If there are any such doubts which remain, they probably concern the "relativity" of values and the "unscientific" character of the usual tests of value. That ascription of personal values represents a recognized mode of value-assessment, as indicated above, and that this mode of valuation has no parallel in the modes in which "physical properties" are judged may seem to accentuate this ground of doubt. The importance of this issue for contemporary value-theory makes a less than adequate discussion of it particularly regrettable. But we must be brief.

In the first place, let us note that if it is relativity of direct apprehension which is the point, then, in these days of experimental psychology, the supposition that there are any qualities of sense-apprehension which are not thus relative would be naïve. The most that could be conceded on that point is that personal peculiarities affecting the experience of value-quality are more frequent or greater in degree. The reason that the value directly findable in the experience of music is "more relative" to persons than the pitches attributed to sound is not that musical sensitivity is a more personal matter than pitch discrimination, but that the tone-deaf are content to accept the pitch determinations of more discriminating hearers, but not content to be governed in their response to music by those more capable of musical discrimination. Valuations may be "more personal"—for one reason at least—because our value-assessments of objective entities are more directly related to our individual—and reasonable—ways of acting. It is also in point that we respect the personal values of others and call upon others to respect our own, whereas individual differences of sense-apprehension do not ordinarily call for that attitude called "respect." Respect for the individual is respect for what affects the goodness of his life; and it is only as they affect, directly or indirectly, the values of things that the discrimination of other properties than value has any importance. Importance *is* value or disvalue. That which should affect the experience of nobody for better or for worse would be the prime exemplar of the utterly negligible.

Also let us note that even value as relative to persons is an objective property of the things to which it is ascribed, and that ascriptions of value in this mode of their assessment are determinably correct or incorrect. If two different objects differently affect anyone's experience under conditions otherwise the same, then *ipso facto* this difference is correctly attributed to the objects in question. Objects having identical properties cannot produce different effects under the same circumstances. If vibrations of x cycles per second do not affect most human ears but do affect mine, what I so hear is still attributable to some physical phenomenon. And if I find sounds so produced disagreeable, this potentiality of the cause for producing unpleasantness to me is a piece of information which is objective empirical fact. My judgment of that is as confirmable as any I could make of other properties of objects. And it is true or false regardless of what anybody thinks about it.

We should also observe that the lesser extent to which "physical properties" as "scientifically" ascribed are relative to personal experience is largely due to social devices for obviating relativities to personal differences of apprehension. Presumably weight was originally ascribed to objects as assessment of the degree of difficulty in lifting and carrying—directly correlated with a mode of disagreeableness, and notably relative to personal differences of musculature. If weight is not recognizedly relative to personal differences in the apprehension of it, this is largely because of the invention of scales whose pointer readings are seen alike by almost everybody. Scientific modes of the assessment of "physical properties" by means of pointer readings are ingenious devices for securing agreement. But "scientific" assignments of the various properties we discern in things would be of no importance if they did not enable us to infer the character of our more direct experience of objects, as scale readings allow us to judge the advisability of carrying a purchase home. The nonrelativity of our sensory perception of other properties than value is largely such convenient social fiction or convention. And the impersonal objectivity of science is largely secured by abjuring all modes of statement in terms directly of those experiences outside the laboratory which mainly give importance to any scientifically determined fact.

Tests of the scientific sort, in ways which allow of and secure a greater community of judgment and a higher degree of precision—*if* at the same time they have a high correlation with the findings of more direct tests in common experience, as weight by scale is, for each of us, correlated with the degree of fatigue in carrying—will have their importance for all of us. And science may justly be considered the most valuable type of formulation for our knowledge of nature. But if science should claim exclusive right to all tests of objective fact, or be supposed exclusively capable of determinable correctness, then the protagonists of science would be forgetting what science is all about. Its importance lies in its demonstrated power to enhance the value-quality of human life. If values are not facts, then scientific fact-finding is a species of conventional and pedantic triviality. Furthermore, there is no essential character of value-judgments by reason of which the manner of their determination cannot be developed and refined in the direction of the scientific. Certainly our social sciences stand in need of such precise modes of value-assessment and value-attribution. I think it possible that the manner of conception here suggested might contribute to that desirable end.

There is another kind of objection sure to be raised against any conception of values such as that here outlined. It will be objected that value is ill taken as determined by ultimate reference to the uncriticized satisfactions and felt aversions with which direct experience is affected. Transcendentalist and axiological theories of value spring mainly from such a divergent conception of the root-phenomena to be signified by 'value'. I do not consider that those who so differ from the view I would defend are debating about nothing or that the issue they raise is verbal and to be settled by convention. Those who so object to any naturalistic theory of values do so primarily in the interest of essential connection between what is valuable and what is right. The sense of right and wrong is primordial in human nature, as is the sense of good and bad; and denial of intrinsic connection of the two would be egregious. To be sure, no one has yet achieved an account of the relation between the good and the right with which anybody else is fully satisfied. But perhaps it will be agreed that whatever is right is imperative in some sense which is consonant with the rightness of it, and that the sense of that which it is imperative to do or take as end is not to be identified with the sense of that which gratifies. Rather, that which is sensed as gratifying solicits action, and so far forth lacks the distinctive character of the imperative; what is affected by the sense of the imperative is so sensed because it does not characteristically solicit as gratifying to do or take as end. Wrong acts and otherwise invalid decisions may gratify in the doing or the taking and even conduce to further gratifications. But what contravenes a valid imperative cannot validly be accounted desirable or good. I take it that such considerations crudely identify the root-ground—or *a* root-ground—of objection to any naturalistic theory of values.

But I also take it that there is no need for such objection. A first requisite for any promising attack upon the questions thus raised is just the recognition that the good and valuable as such, and the right and imperative as such, are distinct and answer to essentially diverse criteria, however the two classes so distinguished stand related. Any conception which would identify the desirable as the good with the desirable as the right and imperative would simply capitalize upon a troublesome ambiguity of language, and solve its problems of the relation between the good and the right by missing the point of them.

Setting aside most such questions as too difficult for even worthwhile suggestions which can be briefly made, I would point out that, as we have already seen, there are diverse modes of valuation—and even of valuation as addressed to the same phenomenon or fact of life. Each such mode may represent an indispensable manner of value-assessment for some purpose or in the context of some type of problem. Indeed, more than one mode of valuation may be pertinent to a single problem. It would be further desirable to observe here that there are likewise different imperatives, different modes of the required criticism of deliberate actions and of decisions to be taken. There is the logical imperative to decide consistently, the further imperative to decide cogently in view of evident fact, the prudential imperative to avoid what will later be regretted, and the imperative to respect the interests of others as we would call upon others to respect our own. There are corresponding modes of right and wrong. To decide in disregard for cogency in the prediction of consequences is wrong in one way, and to decide cogently upon predictably regrettable consequences is wrong in another way. More than one imperative may be pertinent to a single decision; and the most common fallacy in ethics is the oversimplification of the problems of deliberate doing, and emphasis upon one mode of the imperative to the neglect of others.

What it is particularly important to remark here is that there are modes of valuation corresponding to modes of the imperative. Value as contributory, briefly discussed above, and the rational imperative to subordinate, as ends of action, the values findable in transient experience to the goodness of a life to be found good on the whole may serve as illustration. Decisions occasionally turn upon nothing which is foreseeable beyond a difference in the direct but transient gratifications to be found as results of different choices of action. In such a case, the more gratifying is the rational to choose. Also, assessment of value in this mode is often pertinent to some further problem, though not a sufficient ground for the decision of action. And decision by reference simply to comparative immediate values is often the wrong way to decide, as every prudent man and every just man will agree. Prudence is rationally imperative. If there be any who deny this, as the original Cynics did, then I shall not know how to argue with them. Lastly, I should doubt that anyone would be able to assess contributory values, respect for which is dictated by prudence, who could not, antecedently, appreciate and assess values as simply findable in particular experiences.

I take it that the ends of justice and the doing of justice are likewise imperative. It is what is right in the sense of just which is most frequently identified with the moral. But— whether it comes to the same thing in the end or not—I would define 'moral' by reference to that mode of valuation which, for any given problem, answers to that imperative which is taken as ruling, or as overruling, any other which may be pertinent to the decision of that problem. The morally right is what is best in that manner of value-assessment which is to be accepted as taking precedence, in the case in hand, over any other mode of assessing values which are involved.

I would adopt this wider conception of the moral—as against its identification simply with the just—and hope it represents a common human insight, as I would pray to be spared any dealings with the moral man who had no sense of the immediately gratifying or was gratified only by moral excellence. I should also wish to escape any who had no sense for the prudential value of a good life for himself, or even those who should be as deeply and continuously concerned for my good life as for their own.

But if we are to recognize all these diverse but related values, and are to be able to determine their different pertinence to different problems, then it will be prerequisite that the distinction of values in general from imperatives in general should be marked before we attempt to trace the complex relations of them to one another. Given that distinction, the thesis that what is right is to be determined by reference to criticized values, or values determined consonantly with some manner of critique, need not be incompatible with the definition of values themselves in terms, ultimately, of satisfactions to be found.

Pragmatism and the Roots of the Moral

I should like to talk over with you certain matters about which I feel clear but not ungetoverably certain. My general topic concerns the roots of the moral sense and the fundamental principles of ethics—particularly that bundle of problems which is bound up with the currently so-called cognitivist vs. noncognitivist controversy in ethical theory. But as I see it, that calls for a broadening of the discussion to include not only the moral but the normative in general. With so much ground to cover, I can only hope to get over it hop-skip-and-jump fashion. For the sake of brevity, please allow me the dogmatic manner of presentation, and understand the qualification "I think" throughout.

As I see it, this cognitivist vs. noncognitivist issue has as much to do with epistemology as with ethics. It involves the whole question of validity at large, as well as the relation between valid knowing and justified self-direction of our activities in general. It must extend to validity in what we believe as much as to justification of what we deliberately do.

In the modern period, it is Hume who raises this issue as to whether any ought can be derived from an is. But Hume also denied any valid knowledge of what is. Careful examination of the debacle of theory which Hume so precipitated might indicate that the root issue is not that of cognitivism vs. non-cognitivism in ethics but that of cognitivism vs. skepticism over the whole range of human convictions, both as to what is and as to what ought. In Hume's terms, it hardly appears in what way we are the worse off for the nonderivability of an ought from an is, since in any case we do not have valid knowledge of what is, to serve as premise of our normative conclusions. Our contemporary leftists in ethics revive Hume's skepticism of the moral as having any other than an affective and psychological ground and significance, but they do not similarly revive his epistemological skepticism. This is the more surprising because they do not indicate what answer they would give to Hume on the point which he phrased as the absence of any necessary connections of matters of fact; rather they seem to agree with him on that point when it is specifically raised. Yet in spite of that they proceed on the assumption of the validity of science, and indeed are prone to pronounce that word so that you can hear the capital 'S'.

What I wish to suggest is that both Hume and our exclusive descriptivists may be looking wrong end to at this question of the relations between our convictions of what ought and convictions of what is. The question is not how we can validate an ought on the basis of an is, but how, or whether, we can validate any conviction as to objective matters of fact without antecedent presumptions of the validity of normative principles.

'Knowledge' is itself a normative word. Cognition which is not valid is not knowledge but error or baseless fancy. The phrase *'valid* knowledge' is a pleonasm: science is distinguished from superstition, unfounded dogmatism, and baseless hunches by the manner in which scientific conclusions are reached and can be supported. They necessarily reflect ways of coming to conclusions which satisfy the norms of consistency and cogency. And to substitute—as Hume did but as our emotivists in ethics forget to do—psychological and descriptive generalizations about our actual ways of arriving at decisions as to fact for assurance of normative validity in our concluding and believing is as much or as little in point in epistemology as it is in ethics, and is equally illicit in one case as in the other. An exclusive descriptivism and repudiation of the normative digs a pit for its own feet. It can fail to see that only by failure to observe plain implications of its own pronouncements.

I am, probably, a somewhat heretical pragmatist; but I allow myself reference to pragmatism in the title of this lecture as reminder that the normative significance of knowledge has been emphasized before. As William James phrased it, "The truth is what is good in the way of belief." However, I am a little unhappy over this Jamesian dictum—on two counts. First, I would admit that James's 'human truth' subtly belittles what men commonly mean by the word 'true'. It is indeed the fact that, in the field of the empirical, it would be expecting too much of ourselves to require any complete and final assurance in our commitments as to fact. Bringing belief into accord with what the available evidence most surely indicates is the most that we can make ourselves responsible for and the nearest that we can come to any absolute truth. Theoretically considered, our empirical conclusions can be nothing better than high probabilities justified by the evidence; and Dewey's phrase 'warranted beliefs', or 'warranted assertibility', is more accurately descriptive of their character than James's 'human truth', though both expressions are intended to denominate the same thing. Furthermore, in order to describe this character of them as justified beliefs, we need to reserve the word 'truth' for something which may be different—something fixed and unalterable. For example, in the march of science, what is best warranted at any given stage, by the evidence then available, can still not be guaranteed as permanently believable and finally true. 'Truth' is, in fact, a semantic word, designating a relation of the conception in question to existent actuality, not a relation between it and the evidence, and not that character of it by reason of which it may satisfy the norms of justified acceptance.

My second point of dissatisfaction with James is that I should be happier if he had said 'right' instead of 'good', in indicating that character of convictions by reason of which they are well taken. By and large, beliefs which are warranted lead to good results in practice. But such working—good results—is not the criterion of justified believing. The correlation between warranted conclusions and those which work out well is less than one hundred per cent—for example, in the best diagnosis which even the wisest of physicians can sometimes make. The successful outcome does not prove the diagnostic judgment justified, and the unfortunate outcome does not show it unjustified. The normative character of warranted beliefs is not their good working, and good working is not the warrant of them, even though adherence to what is thus warranted has, as its sanction, that such adherence is the best we can do, in taking our commitments of belief, to assure a good result.

My interest in suggesting these two amendments of the Jamesian formulation is principally in two points. First, making them we arrive at the undeniably correct statement that warranted beliefs represent what is *right* in the way of believing. That is even a tautology. And my second point is that the good solicits but the right commands. It is desirable to cleave to what is good, imperative to conform to what is right. The normative character of thinking, concluding, and believing, like the normative in general, relates directly to the right and represents a nonrepudiable demand: it relates only indirectly to the good, and only because of an essential connection between what is good and what is right. Conforming our empirical conclusions to what is most fully supported by all the evidence, consistently and cogently considered, is such a nonrepudiable imperative for our thinking. It is not—be it noted—a predominant psychological inclination of the human animal; and it is *not* an accurately descriptive generalization of our actual ways of thinking; and it is *not* the projected goal of any emotive drive to which we are automatically responsive. It is true that we may—or the best thinkers amongst us may—have such an affective preference for what satisfies intellectual integrity, and find gratification in adhering to what is cogent. But intellectual integrity, like moral integrity, does not represent a native impulse of the human. The goods of integrity are peculiar, amongst goods in general, in that realization of them is conditional upon antecedent acceptance of an imperative of the right and justified. Kant had a name for this affective goodness of integrity—*Selbstzufriedenheit,* being at peace with oneself. The goods of integrity derive from rightness, not the other way about.

If, then, I look to a pragmatic basis of the normative, it is to a pragmatism which turns upon the right, and only indirectly upon the good. And perhaps it comes as near to what is pragmatic in Kant and what Royce called his "absolute pragmatism" as it does to James or Dewey—or even Peirce.

I have tried to be a little careful in this characterization of what is right in the way of belief because I think it might throw light on something common to the right in general.

And I further think that looking to what is characteristic of the right in general may help to illuminate the nature and ground of the moral. Particularly I think that we should avail ourselves of any parallel which may be elicited between the norms and directives of concluding and believing and the norms and directives of our decisions to do. It is whatever is corrigible, decidable, subject to deliberation, self-governable, which is subject to imperatives of the right. Right thinking and right doing are simply the two major subdivisions of our self-directed activities—decisions as to fact and decisions to bring about. And the outstanding normative disciplines, logic and ethics, should show some such parallel.

I shall revert to this matter. But first I think I must attempt some brief and unavoidably inadequate observations about the problems which ethics has to consider.

Ethics concerns itself specifically with right and wrong in deliberate doing. But, as usually pursued, it does not include the whole topic of right and wrong in doing: instead it confines itself to right and wrong toward others—to justice. It omits the topic of the prudentially right and wrong, even though it would be egregious to suppose that consideration of our own future welfare could rationally be omitted in the determination of what it is justified to do, or that in what concerns the requirements of prudence, no self-government is called for. Prudence, as well as justice, is imperative; it is not simply derivative from inclination, but needs inculcation in childhood and reinforcement even in maturity. There is no automatic inclination always on the side of prudence. Instead we natively incline to choose the immediate or nearer goods, to the prejudice of more remote ones and of the rational interest in the greatest or highest good in a whole lifetime. Meeting the requirements of prudence calls for self-government. Also it frequently calls for deliberation and care in choosing, just as it calls for self-control and for deliberation to meet the requirements of justice.

The whole topic of human self-direction in action would also require the inclusion of right and wrong as adjudged in reference to all the multifarious arts and crafts—the technologically or technically right. This sense of the right as satisfying the criteria of some manner of technical excellence is perhaps the most frequent signification of the word 'right' in common speech and thought. Also—and obviously—right direction of technical doing in its various modes is an all-pervasive concern in every civilization and includes some of the most patent problems of any social order.

There is indeed a broad sense of the word 'moral' in which it extends to all these questions of right doing—of the technical, the prudential, and the just—and connotes self-government at large. And the topic of a comprehensive philosophy of practice, or the practical, perhaps deserves more attention than it gets. But let us confine ourselves principally to the problems of ethics in the usual sense.

Any conclusion as to the rightness of doing in a concrete case calls for premises of two sorts. First, it requires some presumption as to rightness itself or the specific kind of rightness which is in question. It is such a premise which introduces the norm. And second, it requires some further premise or premises which introduce particularities of the case to be decided and relate it to the norm or rule of right doing. With respect to the legally right or wrong, this is familiar. For just decision, there must be the major premise of the law and the minor premise of the facts. And this is as true of moral justice as it is of legal justice. In consequence, any positive ethics—any *code* of moral conduct—like positive law or a legal code, is likely to consist of precepts which, though general, have some degree of specificity: the Ten Commandments, for example. But these normative premises themselves require a ground. And to that question of the ultimate ground of specific moral principles, ethical theory exhibits three different types of answer. First, there is the skeptical answer. In morals, it currently takes the form of cultural relativism or of emotivism; in jurisprudence, the form which, crudely put, amounts to saying that the law is what the judge says. The second kind of answer in ethics is intuitionism—the supposition that each specific moral rule represents an equally specific and *ad hoc* moral insight. The third kind of answer supposes that these specific precepts are themselves derivable from more comprehensive ones, and perhaps finally from some all-comprehensive and first principle of justice—the Golden Rule, or Kant's Categorical Imperative, or such a dictum as "Do no act which contravenes any precept which you would call upon others universally to respect."

I make no comment on moral skepticism at this point: the hope is to find an answer to it. And there will not be time to discuss intuitionism beyond referring to the familiar and obvious objections which suggest implausibility of it. I would consider here only the third type of answer. And it is at this juncture particularly that I ask your indulgence of the dogmatic form of statement for the sake of required brevity.

I take it that the Golden Rule and Kant's Categorical Imperative and the third formulation mentioned above all have the same intent, and that any divergence of them would be too fine a point to affect the general considerations which are most important with respect to any one of them.

There are three major considerations affecting this third kind of answer to the question of ethical theory, each of which may be made a point of objection to it. First, such an over-arching basic principle must be empty of implications sufficiently specific to determine what is right in particular cases. The second concerns the kind of minor premises which must be adjoined to it for solution of typical or concrete moral problems. And the third—supposing that we can obviate the first two—concerns the ground of any categorical imperative itself.

It is to this third and final point, of the root of any basic moral principle, that certain suggestions, here called pragmatic, will be submitted for your consideration. But let us try to bring forward, with all possible brevity, what is essential on the two points antecedent to that.

The Categorical Imperative *is* empty in the sense that from it alone no answer to any concrete problem of the moral can be derived. But that is no objection: it lies in the nature of the case. What is required to be fundamental and all-comprehensive cannot be at the same time concrete and particular. The fundamental principle can provide only the *criteria* of morally justified action. What will satisfy these criteria and what will contravene them it does not and cannot say, but must leave that to be determined by something more nearly relevant to the particularities of cases. What kind of second premises are so required for the moral conclusion we can determine by looking to the criteria themselves which the basic principle provides.

The categorical principle cited above does, in any of its formulations, provide the called-for criteria. But it will be observed that it does so only by what is implicit in phrases which refer to "you": what you could will, what you would have others do. And to interpret the principle on this point, it will be necessary to note that such reference to "you" is not meant to be personal. It is not intended to suggest, for example, that if you enjoy an indoor temperature of 80°, with windows shut against any stir of air, and would be gratified with that as universal practice, you are thereby justified in imposing it on the family or your guests. In fact, *im*personality is of the essence of what this fundamental principle prescribes. If your problem is one which involves three persons, for example, then these are, so to say, to be considered simply as A, B, and C, any idiosyncrasy or peculiarity of circumstances affecting these individuals being subjoined to the A, B, or C as part of the premises of the problem. And no answer to it will, by the principle, be just unless it be one which you can equally approve whether you personally stand in the place of A, B, or C. The significance of this reference to "you" in the principle is, in fact, only that it directs us to imagine ourselves as *suffering* the act in question, and so come to appreciate the felt consequences of it as good or bad.

There is no concrete act or specific way of acting which could be determined as right or wrong without reference to the anticipatable consequences of it as good or bad. And there is nothing relevant to any concrete act or specific way of acting by which what the categorical principle dictates could be determined except such predictable value-consequences of this way of acting. No act could be either right or wrong except by reason of something good or bad which is at stake in the decision of it. In fact, if there were nothing by reason of which men enjoy or suffer, the terms 'right' and 'wrong' would have no meaning. And—a point I must emphasize—the value-consequences which any specific way of acting can be predicted to have are something we can learn only from experience and by induction from like cases in the past. Objective valuations—most obviously when addressed to the consequences of contemplated action—are empirical judgments of matters of fact. In consequence, the minor premise of the moral syllogism must be one of two things: either such a direct value-judgment, empirically based, or some secondary principle of right—some maxim or moral rule of thumb—which stands as a precept based on inductive generalization of the value-consequences typical of particular ways of acting, as measured against the criteria of fundamental moral principle. "Tell no lies," for example, is a precept which reflects a generalization about the predominantly bad results of deliberate falsification, and the failure of this specific way of acting to satisfy the criteria of what we would willingly see become a general practice.

Having the intuitionist concept in mind, I allow myself one example which may be more telling. Suppose the called-for decision concerns the investment of funds. In the first instance suppose that this money is the investor's own and he has no dependents, so that it is, as nearly as possible, a question of prudential rightness only. Any decision will then be prudentially right if and only if, on the basis of all the evidence open to the investor, it is that choice representing the highest probability of satisfying the combined considerations of good return, possible increase in market value, and safety of the principal. And, as experience may teach, that is a difficult kind of value-assessment to make, requiring a broad empirical base for any reliability of it. But now let us suppose that this money is a sum held in trust by the investor who must decide, so that the problem of investing it rightly is moral in significance. The judgment called for is no different. In fact, what the major premise of peculiarly moral action calls for is precisely that he should invest this sum as he would if it were his own money and the results of his decision would be visited upon himself.

It will touch upon a point already alluded to if we further observe that the investor, in trying to bring the first principle of prudence, or the first principle of morals, down to the case, may avail himself of secondary maxims specifically directed to problems of investment: "Don't buy in a boom market," "Don't sell in a depressed one," "Don't sell the U.S. economy short," etc. These are obviously of inductive import. The case is no different for moral maxims. "Keep your promises" or "Pay your debts" is a subordinate moral rule which reflects a broadly reliable generalization from experience concerning the undesirable results of promise-breaking or debt-defaulting. It serves in place of a prediction of the good or bad results likely to accrue in the particular case to be decided. Nobody can predict completely or with certainty the total results of good or bad which will flow from any contemplated act. But nobody can implement any basic principle of right so as to reach down to any specific case except by such prediction. And nobody can make such prediction which will be justified in any other manner than by generalization from experience. And nothing can be adjudged right or wrong except through such prediction of good or bad results of a decision and an act so chosen. In short, validation of any act as right presumes a basic dictate of the right as major premise. It requires also a second premise which is a judgment of values, and as such is a judgment of empirical matter-of-fact consequences of the decision so to act.

Our final point will concern the major premise of the over-arching principle. Let us examine a little the ultimate criteria of the moral which it provides. These criteria contained in the moral imperative are two: one formal and explicit, the other contentual and implicit. The formal requirement is that of universality and impersonality. A way of acting is right only if it is right in all instances and therefore right for anybody to adopt in the same premises of action. That, be it observed, is merely the formal requirement of *being a valid rule*, and holds equally of prudential and technical rules and of logical rules of right inferring, just as it does of the moral. The second and contentual criterion is what is implicit in the reference to "you," already mentioned—to what you would be satisfied with as universal practice or as adopted secondary maxim. As a little reflection will make clear, what is thus implicit comes down to two things: first, that ways of acting are to be judged according to their good or bad consequences, and second, that—therefore and obviously—they are to be judged as effects upon those upon whom these consequences will actually be visited (and assessed from the point of view of the doer only as he is so included).

We now approach the final problem—if you are still with me. (That, of course, is a lot to hope.) A concrete moral judgment requires two kinds of premises. There is the basic principle which sets the final criteria of the moral by freeing itself from all specificities of concrete cases and anything dependent on the empirical and informational. And there is the further required premise—or rather the complex set of premises, squeezed into such generalities as we can compass and are pertinent—which concern the predictable good and bad consequences of alternative ways of acting in the particular case.

The question of validity in this minor premise is merely the general question of the validity of inductive generalizations from experience. That is a big enough question, but one belonging to epistemology, not to ethical theory.

The question of validity of the other and major premise is the question of validity of the moral norm itself. Put in the indicative, it is the statement "You ought to act only in ways which conform to all rules of action which you recognize as valid in all instances and hence for everybody." So phrased, it is a tautology, definitive of 'right doing'. But also, when so put, it begs the significance of 'ought' and of 'valid rule of action'. And the real question is just there: Is there any ought? Are there valid rules binding on everybody's action? What we require is what Kant called a "deduction": a demonstration that there are principles of practice which apply in human experience because in the absence of them—without recognition of them as valid in practice—there would be no fully human experience. At least, that is the kind of deduction I would attempt.

I think that this required demonstration can be given. Without principles of right there might be experience of the sort we ascribe to other animals, supposing that they lack intelligence and rationality. But without the distinction of right and wrong there could not be that kind of experience characteristic of the animal which finds that he has to make deliberate decisions and that he cannot live by doing always and only what he feels inclined to do.

I suggest that explicit apprehension of objective facts—in contrast to immediate feelings and findings—is the essence of what we call intelligence. Human experience is human by being for us an apprehension of more than is to be observed immediately. Implicitly or explicitly it is significant of something absent from experience here and now; and in particular it signifies something of future or possible experience. The house we see has a side we do not see, and an inside we could not see without taking appropriate action but may see as a result of such action. For us, everything we see or hear or otherwise experience has this significance of conveying consequences, verifiable in further experience, of ways of acting which we might initiate. Whether or not we agree with the "operational" or "verification" theory that such signification of the verifiable is the only significance that experience has for us, at least we shall agree that for the creature endowed with intelligence cognitive experience *includes* this significance and is universally thus indicative of objective fact. That is the nature of intelligent apprehension as contrasted with mere feeling aroused by stimulation of sense organs, and perhaps inducing automatic response. Perhaps we shall also agree that apprehension of what is more *remote*, and the *multiplicity* of such apprehensions of the possible to verify, conveyed by the immediately given, constitute a rough measure of what we call the *degree* of intelligence.

I should now like to suggest that the government of behavior according to what we know to be objective fact, and not according to the way we feel, is the root character of what we call our rationality. Possession of intelligence could make no difference whatever, either in the world about us or in the vicissitudes of our experience in it, except as it serves to alter the ways in which we behave. That is obvious and inescapable. Hence intelligence without rationality would be an utterly inefficacious capacity, making no difference whatever and having no biological sanction even. I do not suggest that moral and other sanctions derive from the biological one of furthering the adaptation of the creature to his environment and on occasion saving his life. I merely observe that if there should be any intelligent but nonrational creature, the fool-killer would catch up with him rather promptly; and the capacity to modify behavior according to the dictate of intelligently apprehended objective fact *is* one root character profoundly affecting all human experience.

I would adduce a third and obvious fact as a corollary. To

be rational is to govern behavior according to what we know and not simply according to how we feel—that is, to *govern* behavior and not merely allow ourselves to be moved by impulse, inclination, and emotion. And right there is a basic ought, a significance of the imperative. Observation of it is as old as Aristotle. To repudiate imperatives at large is to make oneself out to be a fool—and please note that I am not here calling names but merely using a word in its literal meaning. Knowledge is for the sake of governing action; it operates to advise us of action to be rationally chosen. Not to take that advice is to be silly or perverse. And to repudiate imperatives of action in general is to be *intellectually* silly or perverse.

Having in mind the cognitivist vs. noncognitivist issue, let us make a little paradigm:

"The stove is hot." That is the announcement of objective fact—perhaps addressed to another who might overlook this fact.

"If you touch the stove, you are likely to be burned." That spells out one implication of a consequence of action contained in "The stove is hot"—one possible verification of the objective fact so announced.

"If you do not want to be burned, don't touch the stove." That is advice of action contained in "The stove is hot" and correlative with "If you touch the stove, you are likely to be burned." It merely translates this last into the grammatical form of advice, using the imperative mood in the apodosis. But one who so announces "The stove is hot"—and implies the rest—though he does *advise*, does *not* command. He leaves any rational hearer to so command himself. And he might add, "If you are indifferent to being burned, go ahead and put your bare hand on the stove—and see if I care."

Every statement of objective fact has such implications of

the advice of rational action. Without that, the statement of fact would be pointless and the apprehension of the fact stated would make no difference to anybody or to anything. That advice is the vital significance of the item of knowledge in question, the meaning without which it would be practically significant of nothing.

But—it may be said—these implications seem to be *hypothetical* imperatives: no categorical imperatives here. That is correct. And no empirical statement gives rise to any imperative without assumption of a basic imperative which is categorical. But two observations about such hypothetical imperatives are in order. First, a hypothetical imperative becomes categorical when the hypothesis of it is satisfied.* If you *do* wish to avoid being burned, it would contravene the rational to put your bare hand deliberately on a stove you know to be hot. Second, although we have phrased our paradigm in terms of wishing, suggesting an ultimate imperative of prudence, "So act as best to conserve your own interests for your whole future lifetime," the same cognitive factuality—"The stove is hot"—leads similarly to a concrete and categorical obligation on the assumption of an ultimate imperative of the moral: "If it is your duty to avoid an incapacitating burn, do not touch the stove." Concrete obligations always arise by way of such hypothetical imperatives correlative with the cognitive advice of action, and that link in the chain of derivation of particular duties is always essential.

Possibly it may also be objected, "But why *rules?* Why

---

* That is a point Kant forgot to emphasize. He covers it by a distinction between 'assertoric' and 'apodictic' applied to imperatives—a distinction which is well taken. But to make 'categorical imperative' synonymous with 'apodictic' fudges the point I would make, though he admits that point. Prudential imperatives are *not* hypothetical; technical imperatives (rules of skill) are.

should the government of action take the form of rules?" If so, the answer is that this is the only way in which humans can govern conduct at all. Men can direct their action to foreseeable ends only by reference to some explicit or implicit generality—because they can do nothing in this world except by applying to the present or future something learned from the past, and this is possible with respect to a newly presented or anticipated situation only so far as it is subsumable in some class with past like cases. We know how to bring about what we can expect to happen in the present case only because it is what has happened in past like instances. In consequence, a directive which failed to have such generality—failed to be of the form "In cases such-and-such, do so-and-so"—would be quite impossible for any human mind to frame or utilize. We act according to some implicitly formulatable rule or we do not direct our action to foreseeable ends at all.

In observing this fact, we approach our final point—because it is a short step from the above to the necessity of consistency in decisions and, consequently, of consistency of our rules of thumb and proximate directives of action, above called maxims. We have various purposes, and acting for the sake of one of them often has consequences bearing upon some other. The practical problem so posed has two parts. First, we are practically obliged, by our human nature and the circumstances of life, to weigh, in any given case, not only the consequences of action as affecting a present endeavor and purpose, but also the ramified and perhaps remote effects of the contemplated act upon other interests. Second, we are likewise obliged to consider the relative ranking of our various purposes—to attempt to place them in some order of importance, not only with respect to the relative worth of ends so envisaged, but also with respect to the cost, in terms of prejudice to other purposes, which attainment of a given aim may involve. As a corollary to this, we are obliged to consider our *ad hoc* directives, applying to some class of cases, in their relation to other such directives applying to other classes of cases. It is so that we observe, in relation to moral maxims, the so-called conflict of duties. This is, of course, one ground of the implausibility of intuitionism which takes specific moral directives to be final. As W. D. Ross acknowledges, only prima facie duties can be sanctioned by such maxims.

Our main point here is, however, a different one—the observation that the creature which must decide his specific acts must also attempt some architectonic ordering of his purposes and a rational organization of his plans of action. It is for such reasons that the uncriticized life is not worth living. Most particularly, we must observe that the creature who cannot escape decisions of action is compelled (practically) to look to something commonly called consistency of such decisions: consistency of his purposes and consistency amongst his little rules of action by reference to which his particular decisions of action are proximately taken. It is also here, let us remark, that we see the necessity for considering heterogeneous species of the right—logical, technical, prudential, moral—in their relation to one another. All of them may bear upon a single act, and demand respect in the decision of it.

What is this thing called consistency or inconsistency of purposes, ends, actions, and precepts of action? Often we think of it in terms borrowed from logic, and speak of one purpose or one plan of action as negating another or being incompatible with another. 'Incompatible' is the more accurate word. And obviously, purposes are incompatible whenever the attainment of one unavoidably results in the frustration of another—when you can't have it both ways. Consonantly, two continuing attitudes of action or two maxims of conduct will be thus practically inconsistent when, as we say ordinarily, they conflict. But it must be noted—this is of first importance—that such practical inconsistency of decisions or directives of action is not that of logical contradiction in the verbal formulation of them. What so conflicts in practice may be incompatible by reason of given circumstances, or laws of nature, or some other factuality about "the way the world is."

These two—logical consistency and practical consistency— are, however, nearly related. Time does not permit adequate development of that topic. But one point concerning it we should note. Practical consistency cannot be reduced to or defined in terms of merely logical consistency. But logical consistency can be considered as simply one species of practical consistency. Concluding and the taking of commitments of belief in general are deliberate and governable activities. To be *logically* consistent is merely to be *self*-consistent in this practical matter of the taking or refusing of commitments to believe. To be consistent in concluding and believing is simply to avoid such active commitments which conflict. Don't take such a commitment in one case if you take an incompatible commitment in the same premises another time. And don't deny in your conclusion taken what you commit yourself to in your premises. Don't believe now what, foreseeably, you later must retract, or what you elsewhere deny. Don't change your mind unless (1) you observe that your previous belief was incogent, not governed by consistency, or (2) your present conclusion is made in the light of further evidence—that is, on different premises.

It is just the egregiousness of skepticism with reference to valid principles of right action that it overlooks this fact that concluding and believing are part of our governable conduct, and that the making of statements is even a mode of physical doing, having its obvious implicit purposes. The skeptic of principles of right, if he argues the matter, presents us with some train of thought whose conclusion he supposes it imperative for us to respect, in the light of premises he supposes us to find acceptable. But why should he expect us to find compulsion in his logic and feel obliged to acquiesce in his conclusion, instead of saying "I don't like this fellow's attitude and I find the noise he makes irritating? Wouldn't it be fun to throw him out a second-story window?" He presumes there is an answer to the question "Why be logical?", though he usually does not offer any but takes it for granted. He fails to observe the parallel considerations touching the avoidance of inconsistency in decisions of action, which represent the more general kind of case, of which commitments of concluding and believing can be taken as one species. And finally, he seems oblivious of the point that arguing, and indeed concluding in general, would be utterly pointless, because utterly ineffectual, if it did not serve to alter or modify our physical behavior.

I think there is a very great deal it would be important to develop here, but which must be omitted. There will be time only to suggest the final point.

There is such a thing as self-consistency. And in logic, the statement whose negation is a self-inconsistent proposition is a necessary truth, an analytic statement, and nonrepudiable by any rational being. Why should we never commit such self-contradiction, and why must we accept the analytic instead of repudiating it? Well, *you* answer. I have tried to suggest my answer: because we presumably have continuing purposes, affected by our commitments of belief, and because incompatible beliefs, and *a fortiori* any which should be self-contradictory, must lead to frustration of any purpose whatever to which they should be relevant. It is *pragmatic* consistency or inconsistency which is the final point. I shall seek to illustrate this, first, by an old example of pragmatic self-contradiction, and second, by pointing out the pragmatic self-contradiction in the light of which it is rationally impossible for the creature who must decide his acts to repudiate imperatives of right action.

Consider Epimenides the Cretan, who announced that all Cretans are liars. Various acute logicians have been busy over this paradox of the liar, trying to find the root of the matter. And none of them has produced a solution with which some others did not promptly find some fault. There is no *logical* contradiction in "I am a Cretan and all Cretans are liars." The contradiction in this historic form of the paradox lies in the *act* of Epimenides in asserting that all members of a class to which he admittedly belonged are unreliable in what they assert. *That* act of assertion falls into a *pragmatic* contradiction. If Epimenides had been serious, his purpose in making his statement must have included the intent to induce belief on the part of his hearers. And what he said was bound to frustrate that purpose, was incompatible with the intent to further it.

Second, consider the Cyrenaic adage, "Take no thought for the morrow but catch pleasure as it flies." Any decision taken is nugatory unless adhered to. Decisions of action or attitude are also nugatory unless, foreseeably, they may affect the future—since there is nothing else which they can affect. And now consider the decision "Disregard the future; take no decision in the light of anything beyond the moment of decision." This is a decision of future attitude or it decides nothing. But the attitude decided on is that of having no solicitude for the future—including, of course, any *effect* of the attitude presently taken. The Cyrenaic decision is the decision to make no effective decisions, or to disregard decisions as soon as made. And to adhere to it one must avoid it, or disregard the whole matter it concerns. To avoid solicitude for the future and take no action in the light of it is to negate *all* purposes, including any purpose to adhere to a presently taken decision or presently adopted attitude. This is a plain case of pragmatic self-contradiction, and sweeping in its scope.

I think I may have made my final point already—by implication:

(1) We can govern conduct only by reference to generalities, to implicit rules of conduct.

(2) Any valid rule of conduct must hold good for all instances to which it is relevant. Hence it must be as valid for our own conduct as for that of others, in the same premises of action.

(3) The categorical imperative of action is such a rule—the clearest and most general case, since it dictates only adherence to ways of acting which do not contravene any rule recognized as thus universal, impersonal, and valid.

(4) To negate this categorical imperative would be to decide to disregard valid rules in general—to adopt as a rule the rule of disregarding rules of conduct. That would be the ultimate in pragmatic self-contradiction. The categorical imperative can be repudiated only by such pragmatic self-contradiction. It is *a priori* in the sense that, for any creature which is rational and must make his own decisions of conduct, it is nonrepudiable.

Practical and Moral Imperatives

Within the past year two extremely able and interesting papers have appeared containing comment upon the account of valuation which I have put forward, and in both of these a principal point raised is the question whether this account—which I have ventured to characterize as "naturalistic" and "pragmatic"—will prove compatible with recognizing any valid ground of obligation to others or any moral imperative.* Both authors mention a certain divergence of my views from the main tradition of pragmatism (a distinction made between value-statements and ethical statements), but both appear to question whether it is this divergence which is responsible for the difficulties they anticipate that I shall have with respect to the foundation of ethics, or whether I have merely pointed up a difficulty of pragmatism at large on this point. Professor Browning writes, "Evidently Lewis desires a universalistic normative ethics, but it is most difficult to see how he can validate other-regarding imperatives within the bounds of his perspective." And in a paragraph mentioning "the dom-

---

* R. W. Browning, "On Professor Lewis' Distinction Between Ethics and Valuation," *Ethics*, LIX, No. 2, Part I (January 1949), pp. 95–111; and M. G. White, "Value and Obligation in Dewey and Lewis," *The Philosophical Review*, LVIII, No. 4 (July 1949), pp. 321–29.

inant group of pragmatists," he says, "Despite the author's re-iterated disclaimers of any truck with transcendentalism, it may be felt that he has unplugged an old leak in the dike."* And Professor White's concluding words are: "Evidently pragmatism is united on the subject of values but not on obligation or justice. Dewey, in spite of a valiant attempt, has not given us a naturalistic account of obligation, and Lewis forsakes the task as impossible. We may safely say, therefore, that pragmatism is without a solution of the fundamental problem of ethics."†

In a short paper, I shall not be able to state, even summarily, all that I should like to say in reply. But I present here some of the major considerations which I think are pertinent. In this, it is obvious that I cannot speak for pragmatism generally. It may be that, as Browning suggests, I am a deviationist from party principles. But at least I take as my point of departure a thesis which is fundamental for pragmatism at large: the thesis, namely, that there can be no final separation of knowing from doing, of theoretical from practical, of cognitive aims from the ends of action. Thinking is itself a way of acting, and is indeed that manner of acting which is peculiarly human. Furthermore, it constitutes the possibility of that deliberateness in acting by reason of which human behavior may be self-critical and responsible. That there should be no connection between this deliberateness, by virtue of which human action has the quality of decision and of moral responsibility, and the quality of deliberation in human thinking which marks it as corrigible is a conception too egregious to be entertained. For a pragmatist at least, this supposition that thinking may be corrigible and have its principles of

* *Op. cit.*, pp. 111 and 95.
† *Op. cit.*, p. 329.

rightness or correctness though there are no valid principles of rightness or corectness in action generally is ruled out from the start. I think my critics must somehow have overlooked this basic thesis of pragmatism. Otherwise they could hardly have been so mystified over the question how a pragmatic theory of knowledge could be made consistent with the recognition of valid imperatives of action. They might better have asked how pragmatism in epistemology could be compatible with anything else.

It is just my first point, in approaching the topic of practical and moral imperatives, that *all* truth has normative significance and constitutes an imperative for action; and that without acknowledgment of some manner of rightness or correctness of belief, and a recognized imperative to seek for and adhere to what is thus right and correct and abjure its opposite, deliberate thinking and criticized believing would have no point, and there could be no such thing as truth as opposed to error, and no significance in asserting anything as fact. What is disclosed as true is that which ought to be believed—and acted on, so far as it is pertinent to deliberate choice amongst alternative courses of conduct.

Oversight of this necessary connection between deliberateness and corrigibility in our thinking and the same quality in decisions of action seems to be frequent nowadays. Many appear to suppose that it is possible to deny any quality of the normative, obligatory, and imperative in doing while still recognizing principles of the critique of thinking and theoretical deciding. They thus suppose that one may be skeptical in ethics but still leave all the truths of logic and of science and objective fact standing. And by thus overlooking the imperatives implicit in deliberate thinking and believing, as well as the prudential imperative to act conformably to fact when it is one's own interest only which is concerned, they leave the skeptic's challenge to be met for the first time when it is obligation to others which comes in question. And for those who thus proceed, it is indeed no mystery that they then have trouble finding any answer to the cynic in ethics. They have already given their case away, I think, and anything they can then conjure up in reply to moral skepticism will be too little and too late.

It is, thus, my conviction that there can be no answer to the skeptic which is final, except the pragmatic answer—whether it be skepticism of the possibility of knowledge and of knowable reality which is in question, or the skepticism which denies validity to practical and moral imperatives. This is not because skepticism in either form is plausible, but merely on account of the predicament in which anyone faced with a thoroughgoing skepticism must find himself. Suppose someone were to say that there is no such thing as correctness or rightness of the logical sort—no principles of validity in thinking and proving.* If there should be anyone who would thus deny validity in the principles of logic, he would be unanswerable on his own grounds, because you cannot demonstrate any law of logic without some premise which is likewise logical and as general as the one you want to prove— nor can you prove any truth of logic without assuming, tacitly or explicitly, a logical principle which justifies your method of inference. Any argument to the conclusion that there is such a thing as validity in argument is obviously a

---

* This is not so far a cry as you might suppose. The dominant school in logic at the moment proceeds precisely by doubting what Hume forgot to be skeptical about—that there are any necessary connections of ideas. In place of them, it puts conventions of the use of words. This school falls just short of complete skepticism, however, by the fiction of ideal languages— dictionaries in their own peculiar kind of Platonic heaven.

kind of *petitio principii*. That is what my colleague Professor Sheffer calls the "logo-centric predicament." But that predicament proves nothing concerning the validity of the logical critique of thought and argument. It merely reflects the fact that one who could not recognize this kind of validity without argument could not be argued with. A dumb brute who can be persuaded only by something he can see with his eyes or feel when applied to his skin must be incapable of recognizing what is in question, since the distinction of logical from illogical is not thus sensuously presentable.

Similarly, one could establish nothing as objective fact—unless by rubbing the creature's nose against it—without some empirical premise. And the effects of nose-rubbing might be dismissed as merely emotive. The skeptic who should say there is no such thing as objective and knowable reality could not be shown wrong by any direct argument, because he would have cut the ground from under any objector by refusing to accept any and every premise from which objective factuality could be proved. One who should not acknowledge a reality independent of presentation within his experience must be left to live out his own dream of essences for whatever emotive satisfaction he may find in that. We can live comfortably with him only if he be also a gracious gentleman who is pleased to find within his dream the dream of us and of our pleasant converse together. On what is perhaps closer to the real point, we can refute one who is skeptical of an objective reality, revealed in experience but not coincident with experience, only if we can get him to acknowledge the validity of basic principles of induction, without which no experience can validly be the basis for prediction of any other, or signify anything beyond the content of that experience itself. Unless the skeptic acknowledge the constraint to believe what is inductively supported, he is impregnable to any kind of direct argument which we can summon.

This fact, however, that the skeptic who should say "There is no validity beyond what is immediate in consciousness" could not be shown wrong by argument is not indicative of the tenability of his position, but only of the fact that you cannot demonstrate any objective factuality without some premise which is granted to be itself objective fact, or else some principle which validates inference from given experience to facts which further experience will disclose. You remember that there was once a small sect of people who denied any such practical significance of experience and that, in the interests of a supposed consistency, they refused to turn out for a cart. But this was not, in fact, consistency on their part; what they should have observed is that they had as little reason *not* to turn out for carts as to do so: that they had no reason for any act or active attitude whatever.

The only argument having final force against skepticism in any form is the argument which asks the skeptic to take himself seriously, and to observe that if he attaches to what he asserts that kind of significance which alone makes an assertion something more than a sound borne on the wind, then he belies what he affirms. The one challenge which the skeptic cannot meet is: "Say you are right, then what? What shall we then do? How should we behave, in the light of your startling revelation? And for what reason are we to do this rather than something different? What is it to which we are constrained by the truth of what you say? Or if nothing, then why did you say it? Do you speak solely from whim or emotive inclination? Do you expect us to react simply according to the feeling you arouse in us? Should we, then, say

'What was that noise? Somebody go find it and put a stop to it'? Or will it be sufficient if we tell you that we are not amused?" If I indulge in philosophic incivility here, it is because I do not know how else to bring out my point; and the point itself is, I believe, vitally important. This point is that, as Hume acknowledged, you can't act on skepticism. Repudiation of the basic validities makes nonsense of deliberate action, and also of deliberate and criticized thinking: it reduces every manner of significance to foolishness. If there is truth, then we ought not to disbelieve but to accept it and act upon it. If there is cogency of thought, then we must cry *"Touché!"* when convinced of inconsistency. And by the same token, the most egregious skeptic of all is he who would repudiate genuine imperatives of action, because he thereby repudiates all the rest, and makes every manner of deliberate decision pointless. Any argument in support of rightness and imperatives of any kind must be *petitio principii*, except only for the fact that whoever *refuses* acknowledgment of these validities must then discover himself in a pragmatic contradiction: his denial depends for its significance upon that very manner of validity which he denies.

In passing, let us observe the nature of this pragmatic argument. The kind of self-contradiction in which the skeptic becomes involved is not logical in the usual and narrow sense, because it is not the proposition asserted by the skeptic but the fact that he asserts it as significant which gives rise to the contradiction. It is like the case of Epimenides the Cretan, who asserted that all Cretans are liars. The proposition so pronounced does not logically imply anything contradictory of it. But Epimenides contradicted himself—supposing that he took himself seriously instead of making his pronouncement for the sake of its emotive value as amusement—because the premise that he is a Cretan being given, it follows from what he asserts that no import of credibility attaches to any statement that he makes. The making of any statement implies, as an *act*, an import of credible fact. It says to those addressed, "This you should believe"; and without that pragmatic import of an imperative to believe, no real assertion is made. The principles announcing basic criteria of any kind of rightness or correctness are analytic in a corresponding pragmatic sense; they explicate something implicit in any act or active attitude of the kind in question, including the act of him who would attach significance to a denial of them. By implicitly asking us to weigh and consider what he says and be convinced, the skeptic appeals to supposedly common principles of cogency in thought and argument as something which should constrain our beliefs and deliberate decisions, whether we like it or not. And he also appeals to a supposedly objective fact, as something independent of any relativity to his subjective experience or to our own—as something both open to our determination and requiring our assent.

If I have belabored this point that skepticism is all of a piece, wherever you find it, it is in the hope of making clear that there is no basic difference of nature between moral imperatives and the practical imperatives of any other manner of responsible decision. They all concern our deliberately taken active attitudes; they all bespeak some manner of right doing; and they all represent constraints which have to be acknowledged as valid in supposing that there is a problem to be met and a way of meeting it which will be justified and which stands opposed to some other resolution of the matter in hand which would be wrong or misguided.

I think that the basic imperatives of our social relationships and acts toward one another are such as follow from this fact. And for that reason, I should like to belabor this all-pervasive significance of imperatives even a little further.

What is the rationale of that feeling of constraint which is the psychological index of the recognition of something as imperative? In its most basic terms, it is significant of the fact that all creatures live in time and in a world where things hang together in that fashion which Berkeley remarked in his observation that one idea is a sign of another which is to come. Any given experience has its character as portent: it *means* something, and what it means is not just here and now in this experience which portends it. That is a feature of the kind of adaptive responses which characterizes the higher animals and man. Such a creature which did not feel its experience as portentous would not live long, or be likely to leave progeny inheriting its maladapted characteristics. But the experience which portends harm or unpleasantness, while it may be an uncomfortable or uneasy feeling, is not in us *so strongly* unpleasant as the experience it portends, nor is that which signalizes a satisfaction tomorrow so fully satisfactory now as tomorrow's realization is expected to be. Over and above any automatic impulsion by the now-felt quality of a portentous experience, we have to "move ourselves" in order to be what we call sensible or rational in our acting toward an objective fact which is signalized by, but not realized in, our experience as presently felt.

This sense of experience as signifying something beyond its immediate content is the sense of reality. And the imperative to respect that reality which portentous feeling portends, not by the measure of the feeling which portends it, but in the full measure of it as it will or would be felt when realized —that imperative is implicit in or essential to the recognition of any fact as objective or any reality as genuine but beyond the here and now. And this consideration is not confined, in its significance, to what belongs to the future. No one can recognize the content of his vision as an *object* seen, and not merely as a fantasy of mind, except by recognizing that there is more to this thing than he sees, and that the unseen side is something seeable or feelable, and likely to appear in experience if we behave in the manner appropriate to disclosure of it. If there are creatures for whom "out of sight is out of mind," then their experience must lack any sense of reality and be for them merely the moving picture of phantasms that fade in and fade out of the stream of consciousness with no portent and no meaning—experience which is all surface and no depth. Such a creature could not act, even if it suffer spasms of pain or moments of titillation; there would be nothing for it to act toward or in the light of.*

I shall say, then, that the first imperative is the law of objectivity: recognize that your experience signifies a reality beyond your present feeling of it, and act appropriately to that reality you recognize and not merely in response to the immediately felt quality and the inclination or aversion with which you are affected. The original sin which is born in all of us is the inclination to fail in full measure of respect for the realities signified by our experience, yielding to some stronger feeling which the immediate has as such. That we may so fail of prudence and thus prejudice some possibility of a good life on the whole is merely one obvious aspect of

---

* In passing let me remind you of Fichte, who said that the Ego posits itself in order to live and be a will; and that in positing itself as a will, it posits the non-Ego as object of its action. And he has that other poetic metaphor of the Ego as pondering, Hamletwise, the decision to be or not to be— to find himself an active being in a world of fact, or to remain forever in the Nirvana of immediate and unportending dream.

the matter, and one exemplification of the fact that the sense of reality, though doubtless it is something we are born with, is such a native capacity in much the same sense as the capacity to be consistent and cogent in our thinking. It flies in the face of common sense to deny reality in so many words, as it flies in the face of common sense to deny logic. But our adherence to what is so acknowledged is, in both cases, less than complete. We are continually liable to fall short in our grasp of absent realities—the distant future, the actualities in China, what will be the case if atomic warfare really comes. Full appreciation of what we say we know is likely to encounter some psychological obstruction or inertia. We do not fully "realize" it or "appreciate" it. It is indeed in point that acknowledgment of objective reality is just common sense: where that practical sense should be natively lacking, no counsel to be prudent or to face the facts could find response. But such counsel would never be called for or in point if the giving of full weight to objective fact, as against some more poignant immediate feeling, had the character of automatic response and were not, instead, a constraint to be intelligent and rational. We are born to be active beings, and to act deliberately toward a reality signified in our experience. What I wish to stress is exactly that this objectivity of mind, this rational attitude, the intelligent appreciation of facts for what they really are, is an imperative of our own nature, incapable of being instilled where it should natively be absent—but that it represents a recognized norm of deliberate thinking and deciding, and a self-imposed constraint, which is not coincident with but antithetic to emotive feeling and response as determined by felt inclination only.

One more small point, and then I promise to get to the topic of the moral. In the light of the above, or even without it, it may be obvious that for an active being every objective fact has some significance of the imperative. Not only is there this general and—as I will venture to call it—categorical imperative to recognize nonimmediate fact, but particular facts have their significance of correspondingly particular imperatives. Every fact we find says to us, "If you do so-and-so, the consequences will be such-and-such." Indeed if you accept that account which pragmatism, as well as certain other theories, puts forward, then you will think that the meaning of any statement of objective fact consists in the predictable consequences, testable in further experience, which follow from it as a hypothesis. And perhaps those of other persuasions will at least grant that this kind of predictive significance is *included in* the import of any objective statement. So taken, any objective fact recognized becomes at once a hypothetical imperative. To take a trivial example: When I have the visual image which leads me to believe there is a tree directly in my path, it is a part of what this experience and this belief signify to me that if I continue in the same direction I shall bump my nose. And translated into the imperative mood, this becomes "If you don't want to bump your nose, don't continue in the same direction." Every such prediction of a consequence of action included in the significance of an apprehended objective fact is translatable into a practical admonition in precisely similar fashion. We see, thus, that all truths of objective fact are translatable as imperatives of action. Indeed, emphasis upon just this rather obvious fact of the universally practical significance of empirical truth provides the key concept of pragmatism. And in the light of it, as we have observed already, any antithesis between or even separation of the descriptive and indicative on the one hand, and the practical and imperative on the other, must be ill judged. That constitutes the fallacy of what Dewey calls "spectator theories" of knowledge. Characteristically, the imperatives of particular fact are not only hypothetical but negative; we are advised what to avoid rather than what to do, because there is usually—as in the case of our example—more than one alternative to the ill-advised course of conduct.

There are further implications of this rather simple and obvious connection between the nature of empirical truth and the imperatives of practice which it would be interesting and perhaps instructive to follow out. But I must here confine myself to two.

First—and I put this as a question, since we can hardly pursue the matter to the bitter end—is it not obvious that the practical imperatives implicit in particular empirical facts are hypothetical because some end—wishing to avoid a bumped nose, say—must be presumed to make the admonition effective? But is it not equally patent that any end—no matter what—being presumed, it requires some apprehension of empirical fact in order to arrive at any particular action as dictated? If that is indeed the case, then will it not be necessary to recognize two things: first, that some critique of ends, or justified aims, is a first essential to any theory of ethics; but second, that an ethics which stops short with the critique of ends or determination of principles must fail to arrive at determination of any particular act or even any specific manner of action as either right or wrong? It is perhaps possible, or even desirable, to divide ethics into two parts, in a manner so indicated; and we might well call the first of these two the "metaphysics of ethics."* But it may also be suggested

---

* If this reminds us of Kant, and suggests that manner of interpreting Kant which Paton has recently defended, then we must observe that Kant's own usage of the phrase does not conform to this suggested one.

that what we have just observed could be expressed by saying that an ethics of categorical and *a priori* imperatives, without practical and hypothetical imperatives, must be empty; but an ethics of merely hypothetical imperatives, without categorical imperatives, must be blind. I do not say that my meager presentation of this matter here will justify this suggested conclusion, or that the conclusion itself has been well indicated: I put it forward in passing for whatever it may be worth.

Second, let us observe that the imperatives implicit in particular objective facts are hypothetical by reason of a required presumption of some end—or more accurately, of some antecedent determination of the desirable or undesirable. As our trivial example suggests, there would often be "common sense" presumptions: one doesn't like the experience of bumping one's nose. This presumed sanction would, most frequently, be of the sort called prudential. But I should like to insist that while Kant was right in supposing that any hypothetical imperative requires eventually some imperative which is categorical as the final reason for conforming to it, he was wrong in supposing that all final imperatives are necessarily of the sort which he called moral, and confined to such as concern justice to other persons. Prudence—so I have been arguing—is its own ultimate kind of right behaving. To be concerned for a life good on the whole is a basic imperative of human nature, whose validity cannot be demonstrated without some premise tacitly assuming it, but only by pointing out the *reductio ad absurdum* of all action which would follow from repudiating it. But as I should also wish to emphasize, the logic of the matter is exactly the same when the facts which we are called upon to respect by what I have spoken of as the law of objectivity are not facts about our own experience in the future, but facts about the experience of other persons.

I have said earlier that I think those who postpone answer to the skeptic until they are confronted by the cynical repudiation of obligation to others will find that they have overlooked the valid answer which can be made to such cynicism. We here arrive at the crux of that matter. If we are not to be reduced, when confronted by one who repudiates obligation to others, to some appeal to a special intuition of moral rightness—and to that, the doubter will of course reply that he hasn't got any such intuition—then I think that our last chance to recognize the logic of the matter is in the case of prudential action. The sanction of prudence is "You will be sorry." And to repudiate that as a constraint upon present action would be silly. But if prudence is just common sense, then it is the common sense which respects objective facts for what they are; and that is *not* the same as doing what one pleases or immediately inclines to do, but is the constraint of action by an imperative. The prudent man is not one who behaves like the squirrel that buries a nut, because when it sees a nut that is what it automatically feels like doing. And absurd people who should respond to the admonition "You'll be sorry" by saying "I may be sorry later, but right now I do what I feel like doing" would confront us with exactly the same problem of a really cogent answer as does the cynic who finds no reason to respect the interests of others when he doesn't happen to feel like doing that. This real answer to skeptics and cynics, I am suggesting, is that repudiation of restraint by objective fact must make nonsense of every active attitude and every manner of rightness or correctness; and that is a consequence we simply cannot brook and remain the intelligent animals we must claim to be.

Granted this law of respect for objective fact as such, the ground of our obligation to another person becomes obvious, does it not? The reason for it is that we know him to be as real as we are, and his joys and sorrows to have the same quality as our own. We acknowledge this even when we fail to conform our actions to what respect for it as objective fact requires. Apprehension of this other experience than mine may not move me automatically or emotionally, because I do not feel that other factuality with the same poignancy of first-person experience, and so may fail of full realization and appreciation of it as the actuality acknowledged—just as, in lesser degree perhaps, I may fail to respond automatically to what prudence dictates, because I do not feel my pain of to-morrow with that poignancy I know that it will have when it comes. The principle of objectivity dictates compassionate regard for others just as, so to say, prudence dictates compassionate regard for my self of tomorrow.

"But not so fast," you say. "We thought you were distinguishing, instead of identifying, the imperative and the emotive; but now you speak of compassion. And also, you have said that there is no dictate of specific action to be derived from a categorical imperative alone, but now you speak as if your principle of objectivity made it imperative to act with consideration of the interests of others as if they were our own." I grant both points at once. The distinctively moral imperative no more requires us to try to feel emotively our brother's pain than prudence requires that we try to feel now our own toothache of tomorrow. The only sense of 'compassion' to which I am entitled here is one in which it refers to an actually effective attitude in the determination of conduct; and the other term I used—'respect'—is very likely more judicious. But perhaps you will grant that a little empathetic imagination sometimes helps. As a fact, I suppose that is the most potent of motivations to behavior conformable to what the social actualities demand.

The second point raised—that there is no dictate of any specific duty to others in the mere command to act conformably to the fact of their equal reality with ourselves—is one I should like to counter by the reply that we certainly cannot suppose that respecting others in the manner required will have *no* material consequences. The law of objectivity also implies that other form of Kant's categorical imperative: "So act that you can will the maxim of your conduct to be a universal law." If there is any such thing as right—and repudiation of the difference between right acting and wrong acting, in general, would make nonsense of every active attitude and of every decision and every assertion—then that alone is right which is right universally, and right for us only if it is right for everybody.

However, I do not think that there is any immediate consequence to be found in that which settles the age-old controversy between egoism and altruism. That, I suppose, is what many people really have in mind when they inquire about obligation to others. But this issue of egoism versus altruism must not be confused with the question of universal moral principles versus no moral principles, nor should egoism as a principle be confused either with determination of conduct by prudence alone or—worse still—with merely doing what one likes on all occasions. As a fact, a convinced and consistent egoist could be a completely moral man, respecting others as he asks that they respect him. It would be required of him only that he acknowledge exactly the same manner of egoistic conduct as right also for everybody else. And so far as I know, no egoist in ethical theory has ever failed to make that admission. I do not myself see how an egoist can genuinely respect the experience of others as the reality which it is and still hold to his position; I am obliged to think he fails to imagine correctly the state of affairs in which no one should give effect to any other motive than concern for his own individual well-being. I don't think he could really will that. One of the deepest needs of man is the need of fellowship, the need even to find something calling for a greater devotion than his devotion to himself, and to discover himself animated by some love which asks only to give. And if it be said that, so far as there are such needs, altruism is merely a higher and more clear-sighted egoism, then the paradox involved has often enough been pointed out: to behave benevolently from the motive of relieving one's own uneasiness or increasing one's own satisfaction would neither represent that manner of motivation actually in question here nor could it by any possibility achieve that manner of good which may be so found. But I shall not dwell upon this: it is a persuasion ill-suited to argument.

Short of such considerations, the circumstantial issues as to what specifically is dictated by the categorical imperatives include, I believe, real questions as to whether, and how far, issues which lie nearer to the individual may justly weigh more heavily for his action than those which are remote. Even in a society in which everybody should be automatically minded to pursue the good of others as avidly as his own, it might be the most effective arrangement to appoint John Jones the special custodian of that bag of bones John Jones inhabits and assign him some special duty in the matter of John Jones's joys and sorrows. He is likely to make a better job of that than anyone else: he has the best information on the point and is the person most likely to be around when matters affecting John Jones need attention. There are also, I think, more important and more serious and complex questions to be met when one seeks to make connection between the categorical imperatives and the problems of social justice and of the desirable social order. But that, I take it, would be an even longer story than the one I have tried to tell here.

The Meaning of Liberty

Man has long since subordinated to himself all other creatures inhabiting the earth which are big enough for him to see. And this control is rapidly being extended to the microorganisms. He has already learned sufficiently well how to bend the processes of nature to his purposes so that human life need lack nothing essential—provided only he can learn to exercise a foresight extending beyond the single generation, and cease to squander natural resources which are limited and irreplaceable. Nothing external to man can now prevent him from going forward to realization of that destiny which his peculiar endowment makes possible. The remaining problem is man's control of himself, in his relations to other men. For, due to circumstances which men themselves have created, they can no longer live like predatory animals, or in groups which maintain themselves by aggression upon others. The issues of public morals now emerge as those which primarily affect the future of humanity. If, as has been assumed for two thousand years and more, men are rational, then this problem also will be resolved; but our assurance that civilization may not shortly end in suicide can only be as strong as that presumption. The crux of this problem concerns social institutions founded upon liberty, for civilization arises and progresses by the initiative of free men, freely cooperating in society.

Liberty is the rational creature's ownership of himself. It consists in the exercise by the individual of his natural capacity for deliberate decision and self-determined action, subject only to restraints which find a sanction in that rationality which all men claim in common. As such, liberty is essential to personality. Man is born free in the sense that he discovers himself as an individual in discovering that this ability to act by deliberate decision belongs to his nature. He maintains his individuality only through the exercise of this capacity. He cannot renounce this privilege, and to deprive him of it is to deny him the right of existence as a person.

The concept of liberty cannot, however, be separated from its reference to rationality, as the capacity of the individual to understand the consequences of his own acts and hence to govern them by reference to what is good, and his acknowledgment of an imperative so to do. Deliberate decision would be unmeaning apart from the distinction of desirable from undesirable; and the possibility of self-determined action would be pointless where there should be no recognition that what is desirable has an imperative significance for action. Self-conscious personality requires such understanding and acceptance of responsibility for what one does; and the presence of this capacity in another is a condition of our recognition of him as a fellow human.

The question of liberty can arise only amongst men and in their relations to other men. We may say of another animal that it is free, meaning only that it is able to behave according to the dictates of its own nature without other hindrances than those which are natural and usual to its environment; or that it is not free when circumstances which are artificial or abnormal prevent such behavior. But this vague conception of animal freedom is not that of liberty. Man also may find that the natural environment leaves open the way to his desire, or that the laws and circumstances of nature defeat his purposes, but he does not consider that his liberty is affected by such conditions unless they result from the deliberate acts of other men.

Liberty, then, is not to be identified with absence of impediments to what we wish, or human freedom with attainment of our purposes. Even if such purposes stand as comprehensive and perennial goals of human endeavor, it is at most the pursuit of these, and not their assurance, which could be accounted a liberty of the individual or regarded as a right.

Furthermore, the liberty of man distinguishes itself from the merely physical freedom of the animal to behave according to its compulsive drives by the human recognition of imperatives. Man's deliberation in action has reference to the government of his momentary impulses by consideration of their foreseeable consequences, and his acceptance of responsibility for these. Any restriction of action which is implicit in such rationality cannot be accounted a curtailment of the liberty of the individual since it springs from an imperative of his own nature.

The first such dictate is the imperative so to act that he will not later regret his decision and be sorry for what he has done or for what he might have done but failed to do. Without the possibility of such self-approval or self-condemnation, and the recognition of some kind of rightness or some wrongness in actions done or contemplated, there would be no self-consciousness of personality. If it should be asked what ground this imperative has, then there can be no other answer than this: that it belongs to human nature to be thus concerned for the future and not merely for the present, and to blame ourselves for weakness of will if we allow our actions to be governed by impulse or by present satisfaction or dissatisfaction, without respect to future consequences. To attribute the imperative so recognized to rationality is not to postulate some inscrutable and separate faculty in man, but merely to name a pervasive and familiar feature of human living and doing by an appropriate and traditional name. To lack such concern for the future, or feel no imperative to govern one's conduct by reference to it, is to lack a prime requisite of human personality. If any being have no sense of these, then there can be no ground on which we could commend such critique of conduct to him; merely we should have to refuse him recognition as a fellow human, and be obliged to defend ourselves from unhappy consequences of his behavior as best we may, including the use of force if necessary.

This first imperative of reason may be regarded as prudential only and directed to the consequences of action for ourselves. But already the implication of respect for others is contained within it. Criticism of action by reference to self-interest alone still bespeaks a rightness or a wrongness which is objective in the sense that if this action is to be regarded as rationally justified in one's own case, then it must have the same justification for every other rational being under like circumstances. Thus it is a basic condition of human association that each recognize as right that only in his conduct toward his fellows which he is satisfied to recognize as similarly sanctioned in their conduct toward himself. We might, following Kant, call this second rule of reason the Categorical Imperative. It does not, however, have all the consequences which Kant thought to derive from it, and we shall speak of it instead as the Law of Justice.

It follows from this law that no man may, with right, seek

to profit from association with others, and fail to condemn in himself those modes of action which, if adopted generally, would destroy the conditions of such profitable association, or dispel the possibility that others may similarly profit from associating themselves with him. And by this law of mutual respect, no rational being can claim as a liberty in his relation with others anything which he does not equally recognize as a liberty of others against himself. Thus all men must be equal before any law which can be rational and valid. Whoever would claim a right of action he does not accord to every other either contravenes the basis of all rightness or he refuses recognition of fellowship to those whom his action affects, and in so doing forfeits any claim to be treated as rational and a fellow being by them.

This basic principle of justice does not, however, dictate that it is an obligation of each to act with equal consideration for the *ends* of others as for one's own. If one should willingly accord to others the privilege of giving some priority to their private ends, in determining what they justifiably do, then a similar degree and manner of acting from self-interest may be justified in one's own case. Thus what the law of justice requires is mutual respect, not love: it does not command that the individual be equally concerned for others as for himself, but only that he respect the freedom of others in acting, it may be, pursuant to their own interest, as he wishes them to respect his similar freedom of action. It would indeed be a horrid world in which justice was not supplemented by human sympathy, and in which beings who, by being rational, are able to comprehend a suffering or enjoyment not their own should fail to be moved to compassion as well as to just dealing with one another. Consonantly, although this law of mutual respect is a basic moral principle, it is to be doubted that it provides, as Kant thought, a sufficient ground for the whole of morals. Nevertheless, it does constitute a sufficient critique for those public and social institutions which affect the liberties of men—because, admitting the higher command that men love one another and the moral obligation to conserve the ends of others equally with one's own, still that higher law is not one the observance of which any man can demand of another toward himself, or would wish to see socially enforced, if social enforcement of it were conceivable.

It is a paradox affecting application of the conception that happiness for all constitutes an obligation for each that happiness—at least for normal men—must include the privilege, in some measure, of achieving happiness for themselves and in ways of their own choosing. The fundamental liberty to be an individual includes this right to a measure of privacy: the right to be free, in what principally affects himself, of a solicitude on the part of others which goes beyond the mutual respect of equals. We do not choose that others generally should concern themselves for our happiness in the same way as for their own—unless they remember that happiness includes this privilege of privacy. We wish, rather, to reserve that kind of relationship for those toward whom we feel, and with whom we choose to establish, some closer bond. Paternalism toward the individual cannot be justified by the greatest happiness principle, or in fact by any other which is compatible with mutual respect. External interference with individuals, or with any freely cooperating group, is sanctioned only when their conduct injuriously affects others than themselves.

Thus, in the consideration of liberty, a line must be drawn between the moral dictate that the rational being is free to act only in those ways which he willingly recognizes as a like freedom of others against himself, and any higher or further moral precept such as the law of compassion. And the social enforcement of any dictate not derivative from this principle of justice, even though that dictate claim a moral ground, may still be an invasion of the private right of self-determination in action.

Furthermore, this consideration implies that no positive law of an organized society can rightfully be imposed upon the individual without his acceptance, and that the validity of government rests upon the consent of the governed. This is the case because the law of justice, while antecedent to or independent of any further fact, is a formal principle or rule of criticism only, and by itself alone does not determine any specific manner of action as a liberty reserved to the individual, nor any particular demand of an organized society, as a justified and enforceable restriction upon the action of individuals. The concrete content of morals requires for its determination some additional reference, beyond abstract principles of rationality, to the needs and purposes of men, which are not grounded in, but only criticized by, their reason. It is in point, for example, that the physically able and mentally astute might choose to see a broader field of unregulated initiative of action reserved to individuals generally, while those less capable, or those more moved by sympathy and less concerned for their merely private interests, might choose to see all men restricted more narrowly, for the sake of the general welfare. Whether a laissez-faire economy or state capitalism, or something in between, represents the ideal of social justice is not determined by any *a priori* principle of justice; and individual adherence to one or another such ideal must depend upon the empirically determined consequences of that manner of organizing the social economy which is in question, and upon the relative value assigned to such consequences—for example, the relative value of the larger freedom of individual initiative and, possibly, the greater productivity under private enterprise, as against the greater security of individuals and, perhaps, the gain in distributing goods more nearly according to need under socialism.

In fact, the antithesis of competition and cooperation serves to illustrate that general type of problem concerning social justice which has no solution on *a priori* principles alone, though in this connection we must remember that competition is by no means confined to the economic. A mode of action may be called competitive insofar as the success of one individual or one party militates against the equal success of others, and may be called cooperative insofar as the success of one party furthers the like success of others also. Without some kind or manner of the competition of individuals in society, there could be no liberty whatever, and men would reduce their social status to that of those insects for which the biological unit is the hive or colony, in which no individual can possess any rights because none has any genuinely independent existence. It is also doubtful whether, apart from all competition, progress would be possible. On the other hand, without some kind or manner of cooperation, implying restriction upon permissible individual initiative, there could be no civilization, and men would remain forever in a Hobbesian state of nature. It suggests itself that one empirical criterion with respect to such problems lies in the damage or the profit to society at large—as against the competing parties merely—of allowing a mode of competition or of forbidding that kind of individual initiative. The social damage of warfare, for example, is immense, and the social gains from it are altogether dubious; on the other hand, the net social gain or loss from economic competition is now being weighed in the balance, while the competition of scientists and artists for professional rewards and standing may be altogether beneficent in its social consequences.

These considerations, however, lie to one side of our major question, which concerns the general problem of social authority and individual liberty under the principle that, *a priori*, every man is entitled a freedom of action which is restricted only by his willingness to accord that same liberty to others, and hence that no government is valid save by consent of the governed.

Historically, the cause of liberty has received a major support from social-contract theories including the myth of an original state of nature. However sound the conclusions drawn from such conceptions, these premises are of course as far as possible from the truth—excepting only the fact that the manner and scope of social cooperation is likely to become more complex and extended with every major advance of civilization. So far as we know, normal human life has always been a group life, and liberty has never existed save under law. The binding character of the principle that the validity of any social authority rests upon the consent of those over whom it extends derives rather from the fact that self-conscious personality cannot exist without self-determination; and if there be no worth and dignity in persons, then there is no value in anything whatever, and the questions of right and wrong and justice are unmeaning. A society which should deny this ground of its authority in the individual wills of those who lie under this rule would deny the basis for the justification of anything and hence of itself.

What is principally needed here is an interpretation of this word 'consent' which is in accord with basic social facts. And this, I would suggest, lies in the consideration already alluded to—that no man can rationally claim the advantages of cooperation while dissenting, by his action, from those restrictions by which alone this cooperation is possible and may attain those common ends for the sake of which it is undertaken. Men assent to the institutions of civilized society for physical security in place of "the warfare of each against all," but also from the more important interest they have in sharing the multifarious and impressive advantages of civilized life, which are impossible of achievement without the correspondingly complex modes of cooperative organization in an enduring and progressive social order.

Whoever reaps such advantages tacitly consents to the institutions essential for their production and preservation. And it is further implied that if the individual holds dissident opinions concerning particulars of the social organization, he will advance these opinions within the framework of the social order itself, and not by seeking its disruption, so long as he gives adherence to that general framework and desires to continue sharing benefits dependent on it.

But this of course will be true only when the social organization is one which reflects the general will of those included in it; and no regime is valid which comes into being or is imposed by violence or any form of *force majeure*—unless or until such a regime is confirmed by the freely expressed assent of those who are subject to it. And no rule remains valid beyond the moment in which such assent would be withdrawn if free speaking were permitted. In practice, this can only mean that no government is valid save one by the freely elected representatives of the people, and of all of them, and one whose representative character is continuously maintained by frequent recourse to such free election.

Further, no government can validly restrict the right of any dissident individual to withdraw from its jurisdiction by emigration. Even an overwhelming majority, though they have every right to organize as they see fit, for pursuit of common ends, cannot justly impose its will on any individual who chooses to withhold his cooperation, abjure any benefits of it, and remove himself from the field affected by their cooperative activities.

Freedom of thought and speech, of peaceable assembly and unrestricted publication, are implicit in the right of all to alter the particulars of their social organization according to the common will—and of individuals to further that which they deem desirable, by persuasion of their fellows and appeal to their common rationality.

These and other concrete implications of the fundamental principle of justice stand clear in the history of our Western civilization, and represent the crucial points of its application in practice. These traditionally defended liberties are assured by the basic law of justice itself, and independently of any empirical fact, save only such as universally obtain and may always be presumed.

The Rational Imperatives

In philosophy, brevity invites dogmatism. The purpose of this essay will be to suggest considerations which, if more adequately developed, might figure as prolegomena to ethics. But if, for brevity, these are set down in summary form, I hope it will be understood that they are not dogmatically meant.

Man is the self-conscious animal, capable of self-criticism and of doing by deliberate decision. His activities, as compared with those of other animals, are more largely governed by his knowing, by apprehension of objective fact and considered prediction rather than by apprehensive feeling merely and other affective conditioning of his responses. Man has learned to respond in this more complex and consciously directed manner; he has also learned that this mode of response has superior reliability in securing conformity of the results to his desires. Supposedly, when a tiger sees a man, it tends to do just what seeing the man makes it feel like doing. But when a man sees a tiger, he has learned not to be too precipitate in doing what that makes him feel like doing. Obviously that is not the whole story nor wholly true, but on balance it seems to be the gist of the matter. This capacity to look before leaping and to take a second thought must be a critical consideration in accounting for the fact that men have succeeded in killing most of the tigers instead of the tigers killing most of the men. This ascendancy over the other beasts of prey by a creature which, biologically, is not too well equipped for close combat is the most compelling evidence that rating our human mentality as higher is not a mere product of human self-conceit.

The task of ethics is, or should be, to elicit and formulate the acknowledged or acceptable principles of man's criticism of himself in action. In the nature of the case, criticism is pertinent only to such acts as are or may be done by self-direction and deliberately, since it is these only which may be altered by critique. The attentive second glance, or more prolonged consideration before commitment, is the deliberation of the act.

However, the critique of acts is not confined to those which in point of fact are deliberated. Often what we do is within our power to decide in the sense that it could have been restrained if question of its desirability had occurred to us, though no such doubt did in fact call attention to it. Such acts are corrigible, whether deliberated or not. Most frequently, corrigible acts are done from habit; actual deliberation of them is the exception rather than the rule. But the very fact that we are creatures of habit, and aware of that, leads us often to criticize such actions *ex post facto*, and to take to heart the results of such criticism. We may so decide to do differently on any future like occasion, or not to be so thoughtless next time. For reasons of this sort, all corrigible acts are customarily classed together and spoken of as deliberate. We shall here adopt this less strict but more frequent and more important usage of 'deliberate act'.

It is of some importance to examine the character of deliberated actions, since these set the model for our critique of all deliberate acts. Every deliberated act has a mental part and a physical part. (The word 'act' will here be restricted to activities which eventuate in some physical doing: mental activities will be mentioned later.) There is first the envisagement of something as possible for us to bring about—sometimes of more than one such possibility. In any case, there is the alternative of doing or not doing. There is then attentive consideration, briefly or at length, terminating in decision. Criticism of action mostly turns upon characters of the decision or of what is so decided. But the decision is not the doing, since we may decide to do something tomorrow or next week and meantime change our minds. The "doing itself" is the indescribable "oomph" of initiation, the fiat of the will, accompanied by expectation of something as about to follow. This fiat of willing is the commitment because prior to that any deliberate act can be altered or canceled, but after that the act and all its consequences are out of our hands. What so happens physically has, as a first part, some movement of the doer's body. This is always regarded as part of the "act done," but seldom as the whole of it. Which further consequences of the fiat of willing (further events which follow but would not have come about without it) are regarded as part of the act, and which are spoken of instead as "consequences of the act," is a matter with respect to which our usage varies from case to case. The bodily movement in throwing a stone, for example, will be expected to have different consequences according as water or a window or a human head is observed to be in the expected line of flight; and stone throwing is regarded as a different act under these different circumstances. Characteristically we tend to name the act by mention of those consequences of the fiat of willing which are desirable or undesirable and hence important on their own account, or those which are important for the criticism of it. Also we sometimes name the act by its expected consequences even if they are not actual, *e.g.*, "Tom threw a stone at John," or by reference to actual consequences, even though they were not expected, *e.g.*, "Tom cut himself with his knife."

The consequences of physical doing are not, of course, confined to the physical. The most important results of action are likely to be its eventual consequences for the doer's experience or that of others.

Some deliberate acts are elementary and some complex. An act is elementary if there is no physical first part of it which can be done without doing the whole of it. A complex act is some series of elementary acts each of which is such as could be done separately. But a single fiat of willing may be determinative for a complex act: after initiation it may run itself off, chainwise, without further attention. Also an act so complex as to require some series of separate initiatives may still be determined upon by one decision.

We know how to do a complex act by knowing how to do each constituent elementary act. But we know how to do an elementary act only in the sense of being able to produce the bodily movement at will. The connection between this fiat of the will and the occurrence of the bodily movement is inscrutable. That a physiologist may be able to describe it as some series of physical happenings is beside the point; he does not thereby become able to initiate a first part of it without the rest—or if he does, then it becomes for him a complex act. In any case, the connection between the fiat of the will and the physical happening remains as inscrutable to him as to the rest of us.

By virtue of this inscrutability of the connection between the fiat of willing and what is sequent upon it, no contemplation of an act in advance of doing can have any content other than expected consequences of willing, and none which is criticized after the doing can be so criticized except by reference either to its expected or to its actual consequences. Apart from consequences, there is no manner in which an act done or to be done can be specified, and no character of it to be critically considered.

Turning to the mental part of the act: the intention of it is the entertainment, in advance, of those consequences expected to follow from the fiat of willing, and the intention includes all consequences which are expected, whether these are actually sequent or not. The purpose of the act is that part of the intention (in exceptional cases it may be the whole) for the sake of which it is adopted. Only those consequences which the doer desires to bring about are attributable to him as purposes, but any anticipated result, whether desired or not, will be said to be something intentionally done. The word 'motive', as applied to acts, is ambiguous, even as used by students of ethics; and we shall here avoid that word. But particularly in thinking of Kant, for whose ethical theory motives are centrally important, it may be desirable to consider what is so intended. Plainly this does not coincide with what is spoken of above as the purpose of the act—expected and desired consequences. I suggest that what is so named is an active attitude or disposition to act which, in a particular decision of action, may be allowed to prevail and be manifested in the act, or may be disallowed. As this brings to our notice, it is not particular actions only which may be deliberated in advance and criticized in retrospect, but also such dispositions to act, as well as continuing purposes and decisions taken in advance of any relevant occasion. A disposition to act, or attitude, concerns some whole class of actual or possible actions, selected as having a certain character. And a decision taken in advance of the relevant occasion or occasions is similarly something determined upon by reference to generic character; it is decided to do some or any act satisfying a certain specifiable condition, as the occasion allows. Continuing purposes are likely to be even more abstract and general, and more obviously so, having reference to whatever act or acts will contribute to realization of some desired end. But here again, the eventual reference can only be to consequences, though this reference may be indirect. An active attitude or disposition to act is to be allowed and enforced, or is adversely criticizable, only by reference to some character of the class of acts so favored or disfavored, and to that common character which is essential to their being so classified. And in the end, both what an attitude or disposition is a tendency to do, and what criticism of it is to be made, must turn upon some character of consequences, actual or expected, characterizing the class of actions which are pertinent. There is nothing else by reference to which an attitude or disposition of action can be specified, and nothing else by reference to which an active attitude or decision or purpose can be relevant to particular occasions of action, or can be criticized.

However, it is also of importance to remark that no act can be determined otherwise than as a *way* of acting, even when the occasion of acting directly confronts us; and the difference between the determination of an attitude or a continuing purpose, or a decision in advance, and the more specific determination immediately to do is one of degree only. Though any act is a unique event, and together with its consequences constitutes some unique causal series of events, the total actual character of it by which it is unique must always run beyond our possible comprehension. No act can be contemplated otherwise than as some generality, specifiable by reference to some character, simple or complex, of consequences of the fiat of willing, or of the circumstances in which the act is done or to be done, or of both of these. It is for this reason that doing may be a matter of habit; what it is that constitutes the *habit* of doing is something common to the habitual doings; and that which evokes the habitual response is something common to the occasions which evoke it. Nothing that we can learn to do, and nothing that we know how to do, can be other than something generic and common to particular instances of such doing. No doing of so-and-so on occasion such-and-such is intelligible as anything other than some generality, both with respect to the so-and-so and with respect to the such-and-such.*

For this reason, there can be no decision of action, nor ground of such decision, which could not be extended to some whole classification of possible like cases. And for the same reason, no deliberate act can be decided upon otherwise than in a manner which could be formulated as a rule of action, and—if the decision is justifiable—by a rule which criticism could accept as one to be adhered to in all like cases. And no act can be criticized, and determined as justified or not, except by reference to some explicit and recognized rule or in a manner which accords with some implicit rule which reflection may elicit. If any intuitionist should object to this (no contemporary intuitionist would, I think), saying that on each particular occasion there is an equally particular intuition of rightness in doing, then obviously his rule is a very simple one: what accords with one's moral intuitions is always right. If critique has any criterion, then there is a rule. There can

* As already observed, the circumstances of the doing affect the act done only as they affect the consequences.

be no critique of action which is not formulatable in terms of rules of action. It goes without saying that the rules of any critique likely to be recognized as such will have some higher order of generality than any which should merely generalize the decision of a particular and justified act as a precept of doing.

It is also important, for the interests of ethical critique, to observe that any intention, being a prediction, is subject to criticism not only of its moral worth but also of its worth as cognitive. It may be morally right or wrong, but in any case it is cognitively correct or incorrect, valid or invalid, and true or false.

There is one manner of moral criticism which holds the doer responsible only for the moral worth of his intentions and not for their cognitive validity as predictions. This may be called the critique of subjective rightness. It is this mode of criticism which is in point in the assignment of praise and blame and for determination of retributive justice. A second mode of moral critique would hold any doer responsible not only for the moral worth of his intentions but also for their cognitive validity. This may be called the critique of objective rightness. Objective rightness is the important consideration in determining in advance what it will be right to do—hence in all deliberation of action. We may also note in passing the sense in which cognitive correctness is itself a moral concern, in the broad sense of 'moral'. For a creature capable of distinguishing the cogent from the incogent, cogency is imperative, in any activity which is knowledge-dependent.

Both because of its involvement *in* the moral and for the sake of comparison *with* the moral, the critique of cognition should be considered briefly. There are two grand divisions of decisions which are consciously—and, it may be, critically

—arrived at: determinations physically to bring about and determinations of thinking—our concludings and believings. The connection between these two we have just observed. Let us consider the second of them separately.

It may be that there are passages of experience whose content is confined to affective feeling; but if so, they are exceptional. Characteristically, passages of experience involve sensory or imaginal constituents having some degree of perseveration—appearances or pseudo-appearances, the presented or as-if-presented. Constituents having this character, which mark themselves off or are marked off by attention, have the more specific quality of the present-as-present or the present-as-absent. The present-as-present are generally distinguished by relative vividness, clarity, and the character of enforcing themselves willy-nilly in their perseveration. The present-as-absent are relatively less clear and vivid, and in measure subject to our wish in their perseveration. A content which is present-as-present is normally accepted as sense-presented. A content having the quality of the present-as-absent is thought of, entertained. The affective feeling which qualifies the entertained tends to be generically the same as that which affects correlative sense presentation, but that which qualifies the entertained is normally less poignant and intense.

A train of mental entertainment which is undirected and responsive only to free association and its qualification by affective feeling is revery. One which is in measure guided or directed is thinking (in the narrower sense of non-idle thinking). Thinking which is assigned objective reference, or directed by the query of objective reference, is representational and cognitive. Some cognitive thinking may have no presentational constituent; some has both presentational and representational constituents; but any thinking which lacks any element of representation also lacks cognitive significance. (That representation may be substitutional or symbolic is a complication which we here omit.) Cognitive thinking is an activity directed to the general purposes of concluding and of believing or refusing to believe. It is in this character of it that cognition is an activity subject to critique.

There are, in fact, two distinguishable modes of cognitive critique—one narrower and one broader, the latter presupposing or including the former. The narrower, directed to determining whether what is entertained can be or could be representationally correct and have assignable objective reference, is the critique of consistency, the formulation of which is deductive logic. The broader critique, directed to determination of the veracity of objective reference, or the nearest approximation to that which is attainable—a warranted degree of probability—represents what epistemology should aim to formulate. Historically, however, epistemology has never got far beyond its first question: Can there be a critique of cognition? Can cognition validly be assigned objective reference? For this reason we choose another name here, and speak of the indicated mode of criticism as the critique of cogency.

That such a critique of cogency is required, and must be distinguished from that of logic merely, may be evident from two considerations. First, logical principles alone are insufficient to determine any truth or any probability beyond that the statement of which is analytic, and any falsity or improbability except that the denial of which is analytic. And second, it is not possible by logical criteria alone to distinguish sophistry from science. Sophistical conclusions may satisfy all the requirements of logic, even if ordinarily they do not. For example, to choose first the conclusion to be supported, and then to select, from among known truths, those which, when taken in isolation from other evidence, will support this conclusion as probable, violates no logical rule of inference. But it does violence to the principles of cogency and is sophistry at its best—or worst.

Any critique of action presumes the critique of cogency as antecedent, since intention is prediction, and doing can be deliberate, and so criticizable, only as it is guided by cognition. The critique of deliberate and physical bringing about similarly divides into two: the critique of prudence and the critique of justice. What relations, precisely, these two have to one another is a moot point of ethical theory. We shall not discuss it here, but considerations which have a bearing on it will be presented.

Any critique aims at determination of some kind of correctness or rightness, as against some correlative incorrectness or wrongness. Rightness is that character which all corrigible and self-governed activities ought to have. Affective feeling may impel, and the feeling quality of representational experience may incline, but cognition *advises* our self-directed activities and our decisions.

There could be no biological sanction, nor any other, for the peculiarly human and complex mode of response by deliberate decision, unless that manner of response were accompanied by a sense of the imperative to determine it in accord with the advice of representational and, particularly, of predictive apprehension—overruling, if necessary, opposed impulsions and inclinations rooted in the more poignant affective feelings which qualify immediate experience of the here and now. Emotive feeling and the sense of the imperative are, thus, antithetic.

To conduct oneself so as to bring about that which, as cognitive prediction advises, will be realized with the quality of the undesirable is perverse. Deliberately to decide without calling upon the advice of cognition is gratuitously stupid. And to decide in a manner which is heedless of cognitive advice at hand is silly. To be rational in self-directed activity is to conduct oneself in that manner whose only alternatives are to be silly or perverse or needlessly dense. A rational being is one who is capable of deliberate decision and recognizes it as imperative to conduct himself by the advice of cognition, giving it precedence over his affective impulses and inclinations. Correlatively, every rational being acknowledges critique of what he ought and ought not to do. To repudiate such imperatives would be to decide deliberately that deliberation is pointless and should not rule our decisions; to take it as rationally imperative to believe that there are no rational imperatives; to refuse, on principle, to acknowledge any principles—in short, to make oneself out to be intellectually contrary or inane or unnecessarily witless, and to prove it by pragmatic self-contradiction. The only consistent cynic would be one who believes whatever he wishes to, and for no reason, and whose assertions are made simply for the emotive satisfaction of hearing himself talk.

The basic imperative is, thus, simply that of governing oneself by the advice of cognition, in contravention, if need be, to impulsions and the inclinations of feeling. And this imperative can be avoided only by the incapacity to deliberate and make decisions. This most comprehensive imperative of rationality may be called the Law of Objectivity: So conduct your deliberate activities as to conform them to the objective actualities cognitively signified by your representational experience, and not by reference to any impulsion or solicitation exercised by the affective quality of experience as felt. Inasmuch as deliberate activity in general is something engaged in for the sake of its possible effect upon the future, this Law of Objectivity may be otherwise put: Conduct yourself, with reference to those future eventualities which cognition advises that your activity may affect, as you would if the effects of it were to be felt, at this moment of decision, with the poignancy of the here and now realized, instead of the less poignant feeling which qualifies representation of the future and possible.

If this manner of discussing the rationally imperative should suggest some biological sanction as final, that suggestion is not here intended. Plainly there is such a sanction, rooted in the natural capacities of the human animal and the natural circumstances of human living, and any supernatural sanction would be gratuitous. But question can be raised about the authority of biological sanctions. I take it to be a fact that the human sense of the valid and invalid, right and wrong, refuses to be coerced even by the cosmic process. If that be fatuous rebellion against the inexorable, so be it: I would delineate it as I seem to find it. If the considerations adduced vaguely suggest an evolutionary explanation of our normative apprehensions, that may be intriguing, but I would not use it, either explicitly or by implication, as an argument for the validity of imperatives. Instead, I would recognize that the basic imperatives cannot be argued for without *petitio principii*, but only by that manner of *reductio ad absurdum* of their denial which has been suggested. And that mode of argument makes its point only by drawing attention to the fact that he who denies nevertheless assumes what he so denies in his denial of it, and otherwise makes no significant assertion. The contradiction is one between the attitude of assertion and what is so asserted, not a purely logical contradiction discoverable in the cynical statement itself.

The philosophic sciences are the sciences of critique; that is their distinction from positive science in general. It is the business of philosophy—over and above the delimitation of those ontological and cosmological categories which must be presumed in all the sciences—to elicit those principles which will be recognized, reflectively, as formulating those criteria which are immanent in our critical, but perhaps unreflective, judgments of our practices as correct or incorrect, valid or invalid, justified or unjustified, right or wrong. Antecedent to reflection, we have our intuitions—so-called—of the logically valid, the epistemically warranted, the prudentially reasonable, and the morally justified. There is no external ground for the attesting of critique itself other than such "intuitive" acceptability. But the intuitions themselves are criticizable, by reference to their mutual consistency or inconsistency as precepts, and their adequacy for decision of all cases to which they are relevant. They are also subject to reconsideration in the light of any developing and tentative critique, as it moves towards its immanent ideal of a set of principles completely consistent and fully adequate for critical judgments over the whole field of practice to which it is relevant. Being general, its principles must be capable of formalization. The general process by which formal critique may so emerge, in eventually systematic and acceptable form, is what has sometimes been, and should be, called dialectic: it is regrettable that this term has been so largely vitiated by inapposite and doctrinaire usage. This process is not altogether different from that by which systematic positive sciences emerge from empirical findings, which likewise are subject to reconsideration both by reference to their mutual consistency and by reference to tentatively accepted generalizations of the growing body of scientific doctrine itself. In all his self-directed activities, man seeks to generalize his critique of what is valid, but remains unendingly self-critical of his acceptances.

As suggested above, the ideal form of any critique is a set of rules which, taken together, categorically subdivide the whole class to which they apply into those which are correct and those which are incorrect. But as also suggested, attainment of this ideal is subject to the difficulty that the whole class, to which application must be made, can never be given and complete. As is obvious, the only philosophic science which presently approximates to this ideal is deductive logic, which constitutes the basic critique of consistency.

In the form which currently prevails, principles of deductive logic do not commonly appear as rules but as formal analytic statements of "logical truth." (Rules are extruded and appear as "metalogic.") This fact invites discussion of the connection between rules of correctness, expressed by sentences in the imperative mood, and formal assertions, expressed by indicative sentences; but that topic must be omitted here. We must be satisfied to observe that, as nobody will deny, paradigms of logic operate to determine consistency or inconsistency of statements and validity or invalidity of inferences—and as directives for one who would adhere to the valid and avoid the inconsistent in his concludings and believings. For example, the formal assertion "If all A is B, then no A is non-B" advises "If any premise of the form 'All A is B' be given, the corresponding conclusion of the form 'No A is non-B' may be inferred," and "Do not believe any statement reducible to the form 'All A is B but some A is non-B'."

Any full discussion of sets of rules adequate to the purposes of a mode of critique would constitute a study by itself. Only a few considerations which are pertinent can be mentioned here, and so mentioned as to aim at clarity rather than meticulous precision.

Let us help ourselves out here by observing briefly certain sets of rules applying to more restricted areas of our activity and characteristically phrased as directives or instructions by expression in the imperative mood. The rules of chess, taken together, divide all possible moves of a chessman on a chessboard into two subclasses, those which are chess-correct and those which are chess-incorrect. If all the separate rules should be connected by 'and', the resultant directive would constitute the categorical imperative for chess play. (This should be turned over to the logician, for his ingenious redaction in the interests of economy and elegance of formulation.) It is to be observed that, at any turn of play, the player is categorically permitted to make any chess-correct move he chooses: any such move is right, and it is his right to make it. But any move which is not permissible under each and every rule (or the one combined rule) is chess-incorrect. The rules "forbid" each and every chess-incorrect move; but they do not "command" a particular chess-correct move. It is under exceptional circumstances only that the rules categorically direct just one move, leaving no permitted alternative. It would be found, on examination, that some rules are permissive, whether expressed in the imperative or the subjunctive ("may"); other rules "forbid"; and some are, explicitly or by implication, both permissive and "forbidding." Some also may be categorically imperative, e.g., the direction for initial setting of the pieces.

The whole set of rules (or combined rule) is "imperative" only in the sense of directing confinement of play to the subclass of permitted moves, and avoidance of those not permitted. But let us reemphasize the different bearing of the rules on these two subclasses into which this adequate critique of chess play divides all possible moves of a piece on the board. In any given set of circumstances (at any stage of play), any one of the possible moves which is chess-correct may be freely chosen; but each and every chess-incorrect move, under this adequate critique of play, is at all times and under any circumstances forbidden. (Some rules, of course, may be hypothetical in form, the hypothesis being expressive of possible circumstances at a stage of play or generally.)

Other games—checkers and card play, for example—would show a higher incidence of circumstances in which just one move or play would be directed, with no alternative permitted. But any set of rules which should always categorically direct the one correct move would constitute a form of activity (if 'activity' would then be the apt word) *unsuitable for any deliberative and self-governing creature*: there would be nothing left for deliberation to determine, unless what it is that he is commanded slavishly to do. In a game like chess, the privilege of the first move would then determine the outcome. In card games, it might not—due to the element of chance introduced by shuffling, dealing, and drawing. But if the rules of a card game were such as to direct, at each turn of play, the one card to be played, the game would be suitable only for children and such others as are intrigued by the hazard of sheer chance, since it would still be true that the outcome could not be affected by any deliberation of the player. Only activities whose rules of correct doing leave some element of permission in what it is right to do are suitable for deliberative but right-minded creatures.

One might think of a different mode of criticism applicable in playing chess. Within the permissions of the chess rules, the player decides his moves according to his discretion, with the purpose of winning, which is the *summum bonum* in chess and other games. That is, the player applies, as best he can, such rules as he has discovered belonging to another and prudential critique, and directed to the purpose of a good life—so far as succeeding at chess may contribute to that prudential end. Such a critique of *good* chess playing would be something quite different and enormously more complex than the critique of chess rightness merely. Some fragmentary and hazardous directives for it have been compiled; but for an adequate set of rules to be possible, the game would have to be simpler than chess, or no thinking machine so far built would be able to determine correctness according to this intended critique of *successful* chess play. However, this consideration calls it to our attention that one mode of critique may be superadded to another, in the direction of a single activity or mode of activity. In that case, however, it will ordinarily be necessary to determine which set of directives takes precedence, in case of circumstances in which they conflict. In chess, the rules of chess rightness take precedence over the prudential directives. The aim of winning, by itself, might in some circumstances advise surreptitious moving of a piece between turns.

A rule for making sponge cake is likely to be the recital of some sequence of directives, each expressed in the imperative mood, though obviously they are intended as advisory only. Moreover, there will be more than one rule for sponge cake in the book. For an adequate critique of sponge-cake making, all rules the following of which would result in sponge cake must be collated and connected by 'or'. (We may then call upon the logician to introduce economy and elegance.) But it will then appear that many of the directions are permissive, and sponge-cake making allows freedom of choice to the cook.

To revert for a moment to logical critique, we may note the following similar point. Although paradigms of logic may sometimes cultivate the impression that logic dictates the one right conclusion to be drawn from premises, that impression would be incorrect. It is demonstrable that, given any premise or set of premises, the number of validly inferable conclusions is indefinitely large and limited only by vocabulary. The conclusion to be drawn may be further determined by some other consideration, such as relevance to a matter in question, and hence by reference to some other manner of critique coincidentally imposed upon this activity of inferring. But in inferring, the rules of logic take precedence over any other dictate.

Chess and sponge cake are things we can take or leave. Their rules determining correctness are imperative for the activities concerned with them, but such concern is not itself imperative. The rules in question have, accordingly, the character of what Kant called "hypothetical imperatives." But concern for consistency in supposition and belief, for validity in inference, and for cogent determination of beliefs according to the weight of the evidence is not avoidable for the animal that thinks deliberately—nor is determination of his physical doing according to the advice of cognitive prediction, or the end of attaining a good life, or justice in the social order in which he lives. These are not matters with which any human can concern himself or not, as he chooses. The rules of the critique of consistency, of cogency, of prudence, and of justice are for him categorical—in the sense which is correlative with 'hypothetical' above: the activities whose correct determination is the desideratum of these modes of criticism are activities he cannot avoid nor rationally fail to deliberate. Kant classified the rules of prudence as "hypothetical" because he conceived that morality is a matter of motivations, not of what is deliberately brought about, and also thought that, for every morally significant act, there is one and only one decision which moral principles permit. And although he admitted that the prudential concern for happiness is psychologically unavoidable, he could not recognize it as "categorical" and "necessary," because he conceived it to contravene the one right motive. I class the imperatives of prudence as "categorical" because I disagree with each and all of these Kantian conceptions.

The bearing of the above suggestions upon ethics is, of course, a complex matter, involving much which has not been touched upon here. But I think we can, in the light of the above, define 'moral' in 'moral principle' and correlative contexts. This is obviously something different and narrower than the sense in which whatever is correct, according to any indispensable mode of critical judgment, represents a dictate of the moral kind. To delineate this narrower meaning of 'moral', I think we should, first, recognize that, strictly, its concern is exclusively with what is physically initiated and does not extend to any activity so far as that activity has no physical consequences. We can then define it by reference to the status of such moral critique. The moral critique is that whose rules take precedence in case of conflict with any other rule of doing. That is the sense in which even moral egoists intend the term 'moral': they are egoists by believing that it is the rules of prudence which so take precedence. But whatever one's theory of morals, and whatever set of rules one acknowledges as taking precedence in the correct determination of our doing, it will be in point to observe that application of the rules of this moral critique to our actions does not preclude coincident application of the directives of some other critique also. Unless one be a Kantian, moral rightness does not dictate disregard of the prudential; the attitude of obedience to the moral law, giving it precedence over any other concern in case of conflict, does not dictate every moral act, leaving no alternatives to be otherwise determined, and precluding every other end as morally oblique.

It is another question, however, how rules of moral action, as physical bringing about, stand related to those of correct thinking and believing. Is it ever right to believe without cognitive justification, or to conclude otherwise than by the weight of the evidence? Obviously this question is confused to start with. Does 'right' mean 'morally justified' or 'cognitively justified'? On the latter interpretation, the question answers itself: the rules of cogency never justify incogency. But if we attempt the former interpretation, then the next question is: Can any rule of thought conflict with any mode of decision physically to bring about? Strictly, no. But cognitive beliefs are *advice* of doing. I think that the intended point of the question is as follows: Is it ever justified to allow oneself incogent belief in order to reinforce the affective inducement to some otherwise desirable mode of action? Or is it ever justified, confronting an imperative to do that which violates the interest of some subordinate but unavoidable concern, to comfort oneself by feigning their compatibility? Should the *interest* of cogency be subordinate to the *interest* of right doing? I see no authority by which one of us could answer such questions for another. According to my own conviction, the rules of cogency cannot be subordinate to any other. But to say that they take precedence over rules of moral action would be inaccurate. Strictly, no rule of cogency can conflict with any rule of doing: cogency advises action by prediction of its effects, but cannot categorically dictate action. And, plainly, we shall hope to be able to do what we ought without any noble sophistry.

The Categorical Imperative

The topic of the Categorical Imperative must have a central place in anything I write about ethics. It is also that topic concerning which I have severest doubts about my presentation.

I shall treat, in summary fashion, only three aspects of this subject: first, and very briefly, the Categorical Imperative as we find it in Kant's ethical writings, which is basic for most later thought upon the topic, and from which I would recognize that I derive much of what is fundamental in my own view; second, the meaning and content of this major ethical principle; and third, my own attempt to understand this moral imperative in a way which will be relevant to the validity of it.

I find that Kant offers me least help on just the point where I need it most. I think the shape and tenor of ethical theory has undergone major alteration since 1790. Kant could say that we all *know* the validity of moral obligation because we have a moral sense. One reading Kant for the first time is likely to be brought up short by this shift of language from his first *Critique*—the *Critique of Pure Reason*—to his second *Critique*—the *Critique of Practical Reason*. We left the first with a comfortable Kantian diagram of our knowledge which stops short of any Ego, and puts beyond all knowledge the free moral agency of any self. And we find that the metaphysical freedom from which he would derive the validity of the Categorical Imperative is a necessitated postulate only. But the emphasis now falls upon 'necessitated'. And what makes it thus rationally unavoidable is precisely this fact of finding ourselves under moral obligations and having duties. This *fact* of moral obligation Kant says, to our surprise, we *know*. And if we think to explain the use of 'know' here, apparently so much at variance with the doctrine of theoretical knowledge in the first *Critique*, by supposing that the original German has a different word, and the translator has nodded, we find that Kant has used all the German words there are for 'know' in reference to it.

Eventually, however, he makes it plain that this kind of knowledge—moral knowledge—represents synthetic judgments which are *a priori*. And it may then dawn upon us that Kant is here repeating, in the second *Critique*, his same method of what he calls "deduction" which he used in the first. He there begins by telling us that we know that synthetic judgments *a priori are* possible because we *have* the sciences of mathematics and physics. (This is made even plainer in his *Prolegomena to any Future Metaphysics*.) The question is *how*, not *whether*, they are possible. Scientific knowledge is, in the first *Critique*, the datum setting the problem. But we could not have such knowledge *unless*—. Putting that *unless* before us—telling us *how* we can know science—is the story told in the Transcendental Aesthetic and the deduction of the categories which follow.

Thus scientific knowledge is, in the first *Critique*, the datum setting the problem; and the proof of what follows turns on the fact that without what the deduction establishes we *could not* have such knowledge. And in the second *Critique*, I take it that, similarly, the moral sense and the fact that moral obligations cannot be repudiated is the initial datum; and the deduction in this *Critique* is to be understood as demonstration that only on these terms, this Kantian explanation, could there be this fact of genuine moral obligation.

I do not put this forward as a rejection either of the Kantian conclusions, in either *Critique*, or of the Kantian method. Who would be silly enough to say outright, "Knowledge is a myth; science is baseless"? And who would be so outrageous as to say, "There is no genuineness of moral obligation: ethics is all about nothing"? We may feel—and perhaps we would do well to think about it—that two things here are true: first, that there surely is a human phenomenon labeled knowledge, as well as one referred to as morals and mores; and second, that the complete skeptic must find himself in the predicament suggested by Royce's story of the two little girls contemplating the sky. The younger asks the older, "Suzy, what makes the sky blue?" And the older replies, "Why you ignorant little thing, don't you know there ain't no such a thing as the sky; there's just only the air, and it comes right down to the earth." To which, after reflection, the younger rejoins, "But Suzy, if there ain't no such a thing as the sky, what is it that ain't?"

But the modern skeptics, though they give up the skepticism of what scientists find out, and having discovered that they can't lick them, seek to join them, still do better than Suzy about morals: they *explain* morals as psychological or behavioral phenomena—but in the course of the explanation any *validity* of moral convictions discussed is lost sight of or explained by being explained away. If he would answer the skeptic, one who entertains conviction of the validity of morals is called upon for *something*, and something not to be found in psychological explanation. Just what it is which is so called for, and whether anything satisfying the requirement can be given, is a question at the center of my theoretic troubles. I will call it the question of the *ground* of morals. And front and center to that problem—if current discussion is any index—is the question of any validity ascribable to what we speak of as imperatives. If the answer to that is to be found, we should naturally look to the supposedly highest or most fundamental of all moral imperatives as the crucial example. But I fear it will no longer do to presume the Kantian point of a disclosed moral aspect of human life as a sufficient *pou sto*. It is thoughts bearing on that puzzlement which I wish, as soon as I can, to submit for your consideration.

But first, let us examine this most fundamental principle of morals, and in the first form in which we find it in Kant: "So act that you can will the maxim of your conduct to become a universal law." It but repeats the thought of that simplest and clearest of all moral directives, the Golden Rule. It says nothing can be right for you to do unless you would also recognize it as right for any other if he should stand in your shoes and you in his: the moral law is no respecter of persons. It sets impersonality as the arch-criterion of right. And that, as we may observe on reflection, is merely the character of anything we would recognize as a valid rule. So far it says only "A rule is a rule is a rule." But perhaps we can come at the essence of this required impersonality, in a way which obviates certain boggles often attendant on it, by simple illustration. It does *not* intend to say, "Nothing that is peculiar to you as a person—your taste, your vocation, your circumstances—can affect what it is right or wrong for you to do." Suppose there are three persons involved in the situation which sets the moral problem confronting you: A, B, and C. Let the total facts and circumstances which may affect A, B, and C, and appear relevant to this problem, be set down under each. Then nothing can be, for you, the right thing to do unless it should still be acceptable to you whether you should stand in the place of A, B, or C with respect to it.

However, it *is* essential to deriving any moral answer to any moral problem, by application of this principle, that there be some *other* significance than *merely* that of impersonality which operates. The reference to what *you* could will, what *you* would have others do, is of the essence. Without that, the requirement of impersonality only would fail to indicate any act to be approved as against any other. As reflection on this point will make clear, the criterion which the principle sets for the doing of any act is the good it brings about or the harm it effects. And it further indicates—most obviously in the form of the Golden Rule—that these consequences of the act are to be assessed from the point of view of him who *suffers* them, and from the point of view of the doer only as he is so included. After all, the consequences to him who suffers or enjoys them *are* the consequences of the act.

Let me digress for a moment to remark how easy it is to misconstrue and to exaggerate the difference of Kantian ethics from the naturalistic ethics—say of John Stuart Mill. Good or bad consequences of an act must figure in the criterion of moral right or wrong, in *any* ethics. To do anything except for the sake of *some* expected good would be sheer irrationality or perversity.

Let me also observe in passing that the Kantian formulation indicates that this criterion, the test of the Categorical Imperative, is to be applied not directly to individual acts, but to *ways* of acting, formulatable by maxims. Kant presumes that we bring to every moral problem our little rules of thumb or code of action—settled attitudes as to what we will do and what we won't do—and it is these ready-made maxims to which the Categorical Imperative applies as critique. In his faculty psychology, he attributes these maxims not to the rational or legislative will (*Wille*) but to the faculty of choosing (*Willkür*).

But having in mind the kind of problem I have said that I wish to emphasize—what can explain the fact of there being any valid moral imperatives at all—it is particularly in point for us to look to the question of what constitutes the *categorical* character of this principle. What is the *imperativeness* of it and what does it rest upon? Especially it is in point to look to what bears upon the distinction of prudentially right and morally right. If it were not for the frequent conflict between what will be good for me and what will be good for all whom my act affects, the peculiarly moral problem would never arise. And Kant's taking the moral imperative to be *categorical*, but relegating the imperative of prudence along with that of the technically right (rules of skill) to the status of *hypothetical* imperatives, is his way of meeting this problem.

Hypothetical imperatives are directives validly applicable *if and when*—that is, contingently upon some end in view. This is plain enough, and satisfactory enough in the case of rules of skill. The goodness of some technical end is taken for granted—if and when—and the rightness of following the technical precept derives from that: as we have learned from experience, this is a reliable course of action to follow if and when this end itself is the right one to pursue. If you want a good sponge cake or have the duty to provide one, follow this recipe.

But we may not be so easily satisfied in the case of the prudential imperative. The prudential end, as Kant himself admits, is happiness—in his own words "the sum of all that men desire." But that being so, the directive "If you want to be happy, do so-and-so"—*i.e.*, whatever will contribute most to that end—is a quite different matter than "if you want sponge cake." As Kant acknowledges, the end of happiness is not thus episodic, but both perennial and universal to humankind. Any hypothetical imperative, "If you want X, do A," if valid in any sense at all, becomes an *unqualified* imperative when you *do* want X—and hence the unqualified imperative to prudence when you *do* want to be happy, which is always the case. Given Kant's acknowledgment about the end of happiness, it is plain that the imperative of prudence *is* thus unqualified. If you want happiness, do this, the first-person prudent thing to do. But you always *do* want happiness. So—it plainly is implied—always do that which first-person prudence dictates. It is a point frequently overlooked by readers of Kant, and even by some commentators, that Kant recognizes this implication. He calls the imperative of prudence hypothetical, but in contrast to rules of skill he also calls it "assertoric." But the Categorical Imperative of moral action he still distinguishes by calling it "apodictic"—that is, *necessary, a priori*. That which is "iffy"—hypothetical—may be contingent in the sense of being sometimes the case and sometimes not, or perhaps never. But what is the case, and even is *always* the case, may still be *contingently* so, like a law of physics, and not *necessarily* so, like a law of mathematics or logic. We can easily conceive that our natural world might not exhibit a particular universal truth—say, $v = gt^2$. And that gives us the clue to Kant's precise conception of the relation between the imperative of prudence and the Moral or Categorical Imperative. To wish for and seek happiness is a universal human characteristic and inborn—natural. But it is contingent in the sense that it is not recognized as binding *a priori*. Also it is still contingent in the sense that we can set it aside, and by our free will refuse to follow its dictate when it conflicts with the moral. But the claim of the Categorical Imperative we *cannot* repudiate, just as—so his word 'apodictic' suggests—we cannot repudiate the law of contradiction, though we can violate it in our thinking as we can violate the moral law in our doing. This Categorical Imperative holds *a priori*—is valid in a way which we can fail to appreciate only by failing to be rational. This is the clue to Kant's attribution of the Categorical Imperative to the *rational will*. It is that basic law which the rational will gives itself, and cannot repudiate because recognition of it is the very essence of being rational; and this rationality is the very essence of human mentality. It is simply the law that there shall be law—that there is that which is right; that this law, this rightness, is universal to rational beings; and that whatever it is that is right for one such rational being—the rule or maxim he so accepts—must, if valid, be right for all. A rule is a rule is a rule, and the moral law is no respecter of persons; all rational beings are equal before it, and recognize that fact.

I do not think that the distinction between hypothetical and nonhypothetical brings this out; and, as indicated, I do not think Kant achieves clarity, of exposition or argument, in labeling this dictinction as that between categorical and hypothetical. The distinction is that between the assertoric but contingent, and what is assertoric because to deny it would be repudiation of the rational—that which is *a priori* because it is not repudiable without falling into a kind of contradiction in our active attitude. Being recognizable as that which equally is right for any other rational being as for ourselves is the very essence of rightness. It defines unconditional rightness. He who should say "This is right for me, but under identical circumstances and on the same identical premises, it would not be right for you, and I shall oppose you and prevent you from doing it" would commit a contradiction in terms, because what he affirms as right is contradictory of the very meaning of 'right'.

This I take to be Kant's position insofar as he makes it really plain. And his relegating the imperative of happiness—the prudential imperative—to subordinate position on the ground of being "hypothetical," but at the same time "assertoric," is, I think, at least obscure and misleading. The crux of that matter lies in the point that when the prudential aim conflicts with the aim to recognize the right of another to act as we do, in the same premises, and seek the same prudential end we do—*his* own happiness—then our prudential aim must be subordinated to the moral command to recognize the equality of all before the moral law. The moral command is categorical in the sense of being the last and conclusive arbitrament of any act as right—as the rule of prudence is not.

In any case, it is this line of thought, which might be called Kant's rationalism in his theory of the right, which commends itself to me as sound, and which I should like, if so be I can, to clarify and further. His belittlement of happiness, *e.g.*, in allowing no moral worth to acts prudentially motivated—his puritanical rigorism—I think is really beside the mark. An act which is not aimed at good for *somebody*—somebody's happiness—is, I should say, totally lacking of any rational aim. No act can be right unless it is supposed at least that it can do some good, in a sense which is not merely that of morally good. And I do not know what it is that we are supposed to respect morally if not the privilege of another to pursue his own happiness as we would pursue our own, and would call upon him to respect our interest in so doing.

But having now arrived at the project of my paper, I am aware that the remaining time will not allow me to develop it as cogently as should be done and as I think could be done. I think I shall do most toward putting my thoughts before you if I do not strain too hard for a complete discussion, with every point connected with every other, but try instead to state the gist of some of the main points. If indeed they do add up to a coherent argument, that confluence of them will perhaps become as evident as I could make it by any attempt to put in all the connective tissue and build for my thesis one progressive and fully adequate argument.

I think it is both correct and important for any discussion of the validity of moral principles to bear in mind that the moral is only one species of rightness in our self-government. Particularly, it may be illuminating to compare moral rightness with that mode of the right which may seem farthest removed from it, namely the logically right—what is right in concluding and believing. I think that comparison may be to my point, especially because any challenging of the validity of logical principles would strike us as egregious. No one would easily persuade us of an emotivist explanation of our logical convictions. One who should say " 'X is logically right' means 'I disapprove of anyone's disbelieving X' " would not be given credence. We *do* disapprove of anyone's disbelieving the law of contradiction, in the sense of regarding it as silly or abysmally stupid. But that disapproval is predicated on the presumption that the rightness of it is patent—or as we might say, self-evident. The law of contradiction does not need my or anybody else's approval to be right. And when one says it is right, he may indeed *evince*—give evidence of—

his approval of it in so saying, but that is not at all what he means to *assert*. A logician would be apt to say that what he means by saying that anything is logically right is that it conforms to all principles of logic, and explain that a principle of logic is a formal statement it would be self-contradictory to deny. He might add, if in a bad mood, "And your approval or disapproval does not make the slightest difference to what is analytically true. If you *don't* approve it, so much the worse for you."

In justifying this comparison of the logical and the moral, I can at once capitalize on the recent paper of Professor Taylor, discussing the grounds of obligation in the scientific enterprise.* As he there points out, the common and strictly observed methods universal to scientists, without regard to national boundaries, their common rules of evidence, their rigid requirement that all pertinent evidence should be cited and considered in arriving at a scientific conclusion, and all the other criteria which are familiar to us as the common code of scientific research—these, he says, represent the morals of science.

And if one be tempted to say that Professor Taylor is here using a figure of speech, or drawing an analogy which may break down at a critical point, then there is something else, recently set forth by G. H. von Wright, which comes near to being decisive on this point.† There is not one logic of science

---

* [John F. A. Taylor, "The Masks of Society: The Grounds of Obligation in the Scientific Enterprise," *The Journal of Philosophy*, LV, No. 12 (June 5, 1958), pp. 485–502. This article is reprinted in Professor Taylor's *The Masks of Society* (New York, 1966).—Ed.]

† [Professor von Wright, who had some correspondence with Professor Lewis several years ago on matters pertaining to modal logic, suggests that the following references are probably those Professor Lewis has in mind: (1) "Deontic Logic," *Mind*, LX, No. 237 (January 1951), pp. 1–15 (re-

and a quite different one—or none at all—for morals. The logic of the imperative is fundamentally no different from the logic of the indicative, the logic of simple assertion.

And that point, again, turns precisely upon considerations Professor Leonard put before us earlier: there are propositions formulating states of affairs, which remain identical in whatever syntactic mood they are entertained or considered—the indicative, the imperative, the interrogative, the optative, or any other.* The state of affairs signified remains the common signification whether we assert it, ask about it, command that it be brought about, wish for it, or entertain it merely as a hypothetical supposition. We can assert Johnny swimming, ask if he is, hope he is or isn't, or command it—in any case, Johnny swimming is the signified state of affairs, and the expression 'Johnny swimming' or, to revert to Elizabethan English, 'Johnny be swimming' is the proposition or thought-of state of affairs concerned, regardless of the mood in which we entertain or posit it.

And now to revert to what comes out of von Wright's discussions.† He calls to our attention that what has been called necessary truth or apodictic, since the time of Aristotle, is the

---

printed in *Logical Studies* [London and New York, 1957]) and/or (2) *An Essay in Modal Logic* (Amsterdam, 1951).—Ed.]

* [The paper by Professor Leonard referred to by Professor Lewis was subsequently published (Henry S. Leonard, "Interrogatives, Imperatives, Truth, Falsity and Lies," *Philosophy of Science*, No. 26 [1959], pp. 172–86). —Ed.]

† Let me say in passing that while I should not be in the least unhappy to think that von Wright has fully established identity of the logic of imperatives with a correct logic of indicative statements, I am unable to convince myself that he has. The points which my doubts concern are technical, and discussion of them would be out of place on this occasion. The point which concerns me here, and which I would briefly suggest, is independent of them in any case.

analogue, in any logic of imperatives, of that which is commanded or obligatory. In current vocabulary, the necessary or apodictic is that the denial of which is itself a logical contradiction; correlatively, the *not*-necessary is that which *can* be denied without self-contradiction. The *logically interdicted,* the *absurdum* of the *reductio ad absurdum* in geometry and elsewhere, is that which explicitly or by implication is contradictory, inconsistent in itself—logically impossible; and that which is not thus absurd—the noncontradictory, the logically possible—is that which, whether true or false, is self-consistent. All these ideas are definable in terms of two: "self-consistent" and "false."

$\sim$ p: not-p, denial of p

$\Diamond$ p: p self-consistent; (logically) permissible (to suppose)

$\Diamond \sim$ p: p (logically) permissible to deny

$\sim \Diamond$ p: p (logically) impermissible to affirm

$\sim \Diamond \sim$ p: p not (logically) permissible to deny; necessary; apodictic

q inferable from p: (logically) impermissible to affirm p and deny q

$p < q: = Df. \sim \Diamond (p \sim q) \ [= p \sim q. < .p \sim p]$

Logic is traditionally called normative. Supposedly it represents a critique of our conclusions, the sanction of deductive inferences and the interdiction of fallacious steps of proof. The elenchus of valid deduction is a relation '$p < q$' ('q is inferable from p') such that '$p \sim q$' is self-inconsistent. To admit 'p' but deny 'q' is a contradiction, an inconsistency. If we admit the premise 'p', then we are in consistency bound to admit also the logical consequence 'q'. That is logically commanded. Inconsistency is logically forbidden. What is not logically forbidden, it is logically permissible to suppose;

and what is not commanded is—so far as logic goes—permissible to suppose false.

The analogy to the imperative at large, and of the four modes respectively to the commanded or imperative in general, the forbidden or interdicted, the permissible to adopt, and the permissible to omit or avoid, will be obvious.

And now one more point. Logic is not usually written in the imperative mood. But please note: '$\sim \Diamond \sim p$', which expresses the status of the logically obligatory, is exactly that the denial of which is '$\Diamond \sim p$'. It says also, 'It is (logically) impermissible to deny p'. In such case, '$\sim p$' is self-contradictory and reducible to some statement of the form 'p $\sim$ p'. In other words, '$\sim \Diamond \sim p$' says, in current vocabulary, 'p is analytic'. And however divergent in form, there could be *no* valid logic of propositions which should assert either as assumptions or as derived theorems any statement which is not analytic. This necessary or analytic character of its assertions might well be taken as a definitive requirement of anything called logic. For the rest, according to prevailing theory, logic can be marked off only by reference to the restricted vocabulary in which it is formulated. For example, in contemporary truth-value logic—*e.g.,* the early sections of *Principia Mathematica*—the idea of consistency, here symbolized by ' $\Diamond$ p', is not included—Mr. Russell has said "for reasons of economy" —in the vocabulary, and the modal qualifications are unexpressed. But in *Principia*—unless for a few misprints—there is *no postulate* which is *not analytic, no line of proof* which is not analytic, and *no theorem* which is not analytic. And unless Mr. Russell has changed his mind since I last heard, he would repudiate as invalid anything printed in *Principia* after the symbol of assertion, if he became convinced that what it says is not analytic.

If what I have thus drawn from consideration of von Wright, or modal logic, is correct, then it becomes obvious that the whole imperative force of logic can be summed up in one directive: "Be consistent: accept what in consistency you are bound to admit, and avoid commitment to anything which would be, explicitly or by implication, contradictory." Being thus consistent is the minimum requirement for avoiding commitment to what is false in the determination of beliefs, and is the *sine qua non* of rationality in thinking.

It strongly suggests itself that this logic of the imperative in concluding and believing may extend also to the imperative in doing. Insofar as doing is subject to any critique, is something which we justify or criticize, and consider right or wrong, there must be directives of it; and there must be something to be labeled (in quotation marks) the "logic" of decisions to do as there is a logic of decisions of belief. It is the suggestion of von Wright's work that this logic is at the root uniform in the two cases, and that this logic is statable in terms of the permissible, the impermissible, the permissible to omit or repudiate, and the impermissible to repudiate, the commanded.

Again, I revert to Mr. Leonard's paper—though this time with a touch of misgiving; he may take exception to my present suggestion. Any doing is a bringing about of some state of affairs, and the making true of some contingent proposition. But the making true of any proposition cannot fail to be governed, and the possibility of it governed, by the necessary connections, the logical connections, of that proposition. Any contemplated bringing about, any plan of action which is rational, if it is to be a well-considered plan, must be observant of the logical relations in which the states of affairs involved, the propositions contemplated in this mood of "to be brought about" stand related. Any logic, by portraying necessary connections of contemplated states of affairs or propositions, cannot fail to be included in the critique of any rational decision to do.

The vistas so opened out lead in several directions and, as I am sure you will see at once, raise numerous and complex questions. I am sure that I do not see as far into these as is called for. Even what I seem to discern, I should hesitate to put before you—and could not do so within the scope of this lecture in any case.

There is also, in this suggested parallel between the logic of principles of the right in a rational determination of beliefs and a logic of right or justified decisions to do, that which must strongly remind us of Kant, and especially of that dominant strain in his ethics which I have called his rationalism. It is an old thought that what the Categorical Imperative demands is nothing more than consistency in doing, or more accurately, consistency in our accepted directives of doing—Kant's maxims.

If we reflect upon what the Categorical Imperative in fact requires, we may surprise ourselves by discovering that, though in one sense it demands so much and is a counsel of perfection, in another sense it demands so little. Even the emotivist could line up under this rubric, and recognize the Categorical Imperative as implicit in his interpretation of right and wrong. If "X is right" means "I approve of X as a way of doing or an active attitude; do so as well," the same canon of self-criticism is implicit as in the Golden Rule: "Approve only of such doing as you would have others likewise approve." The emotivist must be careful of his approvings and disapprovings lest this emotive contagion of them which he seeks to promote should have consequences—to himself perhaps—which will make him sorry and of which he will then *disapprove.*

For example, he may approve of stockpiling atom bombs—or of *not* stockpiling atom bombs—and seek the agreement of others. But whichever attitude on this issue he now approves—and of course he is certain what his own present attitude is, if he has any—does that settle the point he wants to settle? He, too, must recognize a *constraint not* to approve too impulsively or from any emotive drive or transient inclination without this thought: "What if others should do likewise or should share my approval?" It is even a reasonable extrapolation, which he could hardly refuse, to go the whole length and phrase it: "Approve only of what you could will to be universally approved." And that is just what the Categorical Imperative says. It does not even rule out the affective or emotive as the ground of "what you could will." Indeed Kant himself recognizes that; the *Willkür* which lies at the root of our maxims he ascribes, not to reason or understanding, but to the *Begehrungsvermögen,* the faculty of desire. He merely emphasizes this implicit *constraint upon the emotive* of a rational critique by reference to envisaging what would happen if everybody approved of the way of acting to which your affective feeling moves you to give rein. And he emphasizes this *constraint* as not itself emotively instigated. Instead, and like Aristotle, he takes that to be rooted in rationality whose function it is to *govern* the emotive propensities. If the emotivist in ethics follow out this implication of his hortation "Do you so likewise," conceivably he might recognize himself as a good Kantian in ethics. His remaining question might be: But which is boss—the affective instigation or the implicit constraint by reference to the possible universalization of the same attitude?

The egoist too, if he be a philosophical egoist, and not merely an unreflective and impulsive one, promulgates his doctrine of the exclusive rule of first-person prudence with eyes wide open. He is prepared to admit that the rule of right which he proposes is equally justified in the case of any other as in his own. He merely disagrees as to the maxim he declares himself prepared to see universalized and become the unexceptionable directive of everybody's conduct. He may delude himself about the consequences of that, and Kant apparently did not expect any reasonable animal to favor universal egoism, but there is nothing in the Categorical Imperative to rule it out, unless it be in a reasonable expectation of the consequences of unadulterated egoism as universal practice.

But what is it, in any logic of doing, that could be the counterpart of consistency in the logic of believing and concluding? I would suggest that it may be something which lies in the nature of deliberate action itself. All deliberate action is governed by expectation of results. That is what the fiat of the will, the commitment of action, commits itself to—the expected consequences. That is the *content* of the decision to do, and that for the sake of which the act is done. The consistency of action lies in the acceptability of the consequences you expect and commit yourself to by doing, when these consequences are brought home to you by being realized. Failure of the consequences to be what you anticipate and will is a limitation of intelligence, but knowing the better and doing the worse is a failure to act rationally, a failure of self-government.

And this is not so different in the case of concluding and believing and in the case of action. It belongs to the nature of believing that it attempts to envisage what will be verifiable, and the belief we now accept is both accepted for the sake of its predictive signification and accepted only through expectation that what is believed now will be similarly acceptable in the future. That indeed represents the vital function of believing—to anticipate now what will be later verifiable. The truth is merely the ideal of a belief we need never retract. Accord of commitment taken now with what we shall later find it acceptable to remain committed to is the ultimate sanction both of believing and of doing. And for the creature who decides his believing and his doing, and with reference to the expected future which will test the worth of his believing or his doing, a major precept to which by his nature as deliberate believer and doer he is constrained is "So far as in you lies, take no commitment now which later you will be dissatisfied to have taken, to have believed or to have done." Respect for that imperative is, I suggest, of the essence of what we call our rationality.

There is much I must omit here, particularly what pertains to morals in the distinctive sense of governing our conduct in relation to our fellows. I permit myself only a final suggestion relevant to the nonrepudiability of the ultimately imperative, whether in believing and concluding, or in doing. We have a passion for proving, but we have to recognize that for first principles, whether of logic or morals, there can be no proof. Any attempt to demonstrate first principles of logic would inevitably be *petitio principii*. Not only must it assume some first principles as premises, but in deriving any further principles it must find sanction for steps taken in these same first premises now utilized as rules of derivation—rules of derivation *which are accepted as valid*. Any proof in logic must thus doubly beg the question.

But, by the same token, any argument against objective validity in the type of principles called logical must reduce itself to absurdity. One who argues either presumes that there is a certain consequentiality between his premises and his conclusion which we shall find it imperative to respect, and by reason of which, having admitted his premises, we are bound to admit his conclusion, or—failing that admission—he must relinquish all claim upon our attention. So to say, his act of arguing belies his skeptical conclusion, by witnessing that he presumes in his active assertion what he denies in words. Whoever confesses himself insouciant to consistency rules himself out of any forum, as Epimenides ruled out the possibility of taking him seriously when, being a Cretan, he said that all Cretans are liars.

I have no desire to rehash this timeworn paradox of the liar. I would only suggest that the perennial failure to produce a solution of it—one which fully satisfies anybody but the author —may lie in the fact that the Epimenidean inconsistency does *not* turn upon any contradiction of the propositions involved. If someone else in the courtroom should have said, "Epimenides is a Cretan, and all Cretans are liars," it would have been a self-consistent statement and conceivably plausible. But when *Epimenides* says or implies that *he* is a liar, he discredits any statement he may make. The inconsistency involved is not discoverable as a relation of propositions asserted or implied; it is an inconsistency between the content of assertion and the act of asserting it—in Mr. Leonard's language, an inconsistency involved in using the words "I am a liar," or any which logically imply that, as a *deliberate sign*. As deliberate, and to be understood as deliberate, this act of assertion conveys the intent that what is said should be believed. But the content of the assertion made—the state of affairs it affirms to be actual— is one in which this assertor's assertions are not to be believed on the evidence of his making them. The act is self-frustrating of its own ostensive purpose. That I shall call a pragmatic contradiction.

As already pointed out, one who denies the validity of the imperative of *logical* principles falls into this manner of predicament; he would implicitly assert that no statement made or believed constrains us to believe any so-called logical consequence of it, as against any rival assertion, including what it contradicts. He makes argumentative sentences—to himself if not to any other—which if taken to be true would have the consequence of vitiating any purpose in making argumentative sentences, or any purpose of entertaining in his own mind any train of thought with the purpose of so determining his beliefs. If he turns his skepticism on the train of thought leading to his own skeptical conclusion, he convicts himself of being silly in believing the conclusion of it. So much for denying validity to logical principles.

I wish to suggest briefly that one who denies the validity of other imperatives of rationality likewise falls into this predicament of pragmatic contradiction.

Take the imperative of prudence, which the Cyrenaic derides, saying, "Take no thought for the morrow; catch pleasure as it flies; gratify every momentary impulse, so far as you can; never subordinate any good of the moment from concern for a later good." Be it noted, he is recommending a comprehensive and continuing attitude toward life, a principle of action. And the principle he recommends is that each future moment be faced with the intent to repudiate all inhibitions or constraints upon its momentary impulse or inclination. But the ostensive purpose of his present resolution—the resolution he recommends—implies that it is pointless to bother about the future and make any resolution at all with the intent to constrain it in any way. He exhorts us to take this thought as a continuing counsel—the thought, namely, that we should never bother ourselves about the future. But *he is* bothering himself about the future, because there is nothing but the future which any exhortation—to oneself or anybody else— could affect. His act of exhorting belies the content of his exhortation—or of any other exhortation. *Any* act is directed to the future. "Have no regard for the future; be unconstrained by any consideration of the future" has the implication "Do no acts for a purpose; take no active attitudes." But here is this silly fellow taking one and recommending it to others. Presumably, like Epimenides, he speaks for his own present amusement—and theirs.

And now, what about Kant's Categorical Imperative? I have left myself totally insufficient time for anything beyond a few observations, dogmatically stated. As already indicated, I do *not* think that it dictates universal benevolence. I have often wondered whether Kant did. Not only could any philosophical egoist crawl under the Kantian tent—if he be as tough as he thinks he is and is really prepared to take the consequences; but I also think one who should say, "I will put my own interests first in the family, my family first in the town, my town first in the country, and my country first in the world," could also join the company—again, provided he is tough enough to take it, at each of these suggested stages. But I suggest that if he does think this is—at each stage—the recipe for the happy life he seeks, he is likely to be disappointed by the mess he will so cook up for himself. Perhaps the first step of dominating the family will suggest that. But the main theoretic point is that I do not believe that Kant's Categorical Imperative affords sufficient ground by itself for any specific and positive code of social conduct. We read into it our own, whatever it be; and that is exactly what the statement of it invites.

What it says is only this: whatever code of conduct you think is the one to which you ought to adhere must also be that to which you think any fellow of yours ought to adhere. But please notice, I still say "code," and do not refer to acts. As already indicated, reference to specific acts calls for the added proviso "in the same premises of action." Kant is, I think, abundantly right in presuming that it is formulatable *ways* of acting, maxims, subordinate but still general rules, which are the subject matter which the Categorical Imperative may operate upon as critique.

Also, I invite observation of the fact that this Categorical Imperative applies to the activities of thinking and concluding. Regard no conclusion as valid for you unless you could regard it as the valid conclusion for any rational being to draw: believe nothing that you would think it wrong for any other rational being to believe, in the same premises.

What the Categorical Imperative says is no more than that there is a nonrepudiable distinction between right and wrong, which affects whatever we must decide by deliberation. And this distinction *is* nonrepudiable for any creature who thinks, and thinks to a purpose, and is called upon to decide by thinking. There is the moral imperative because, important amongst things the rational animal must decide, there is the question how he shall behave toward his fellows. And any creature who talks to himself about that will find himself in the predicament of pragmatic contradiction if he says to himself that there is a way of acting which is right for him but wrong, in the same premises of action, for another creature who likewise decides by talking to himself. He can only escape the Categorical Imperative by repudiating the significance of deciding by such deliberation. The validity of thinking is not finally separable from the validity of deliberate doing, because the deliberation is itself a manner of doing, and the deliberate doing is its characteristic and determined consequence.

The skeptic of valid imperatives can never hope to convince that other self which lives with all of us, observant of what we think and what we do, and may, on occasion, refuse to be convinced of what we think, and disapprove of what we do. The self-conscious being must live with himself in time, and he who is given to critical second-thinking must strive to be consistent and win his own more than temporary approval.